POLITICAL LEADER

SWAT PAT

LONDON SCHOOL OF ECONOMICS
MONOGRAPHS ON SOCIAL ANTHROPOLOGY

Managing Editor: J. P. Parry

The Monographs on Social Anthropology were established in 1940 and aim to publish results of modern anthropological research of primary interest to specialists.

The continuation of the series was made possible by a grant in aid from the Wenner-Gren Foundation for Anthropological Research, and more recently by a further grant from the Governors of the London School of Economics and Political Science.

The Monographs are under the direction of an Editorial Board associated with the Department of Anthropology of the London School of Economics and Political Science.

LONDON SCHOOL OF ECONOMICS
MONOGRAPHS ON SOCIAL ANTHROPOLOGY
No. 19

Political Leadership among Swat Pathans

by

FREDRIK BARTH

THE ATHLONE PRESS
NEW YORK: HUMANITIES PRESS INC.

Published by
THE ATHLONE PRESS
at 90-91 *Great Russell Street, London* WC1
The Athlone Press is an imprint of
Bemrose UK Ltd

© *Fredrik Barth,* 1959, 1965

ISBN 0 485 19619 0

Library of Congress Catalog Card No. 65-16342

First edition 1959
First paperback edition, with corrections 1965
Reprinted 1970, 1972, 1975, 1980

Printed and bound by
REDWOOD BURN LIMITED
Trowbridge and Esher

Preface

THE PRESENT STUDY describes certain aspects of the society of the Pathans of the Swat valley in the North-West Frontier Province of Pakistan. Except where other reference is given, the material on which it is based was collected by the author in the period February-November 1954. The fieldwork was financed by a grant from the Royal Norwegian Research Council. The analysis of the material has been aided by a Wenner-Gren Pre-doctoral Fellowship.

Thanks to the patient teaching of Professor Morgenstierne of the University of Oslo during the year preceding fieldwork, I was able to start shortly after my arrival to speak and work in the Pashto language. In the beginning of fieldwork, moreover, I was greatly aided by Ayub Khan of Thana, who served as my interpreter for two months.

I am greatly indebted to H.R.H. the Wali of Swat, who took a positive interest in this study, and to his various administrative officials, most particularly the Chief Secretary, who assisted me in every way. But their help would have availed little had I not been hospitably received by a great number of Pathans in all walks of life. They became my friends, and by their explanations and example contributed to my understanding of their society. I should particularly mention my servant Kashmali. To defend his own and his master's prestige, he carefully coached me in etiquette, explained the labyrinth of friendship and enmity between the persons I met, and thus contributed greatly both to my success with others and to my knowledge of the area.

In the analysis of this material, I have been aided by discussions with friends and colleagues in Oslo, London and Manchester. But most of all I wish to acknowledge my debts to the staff and fellow students of the Faculty of Anthropology in Cambridge for formal and informal instruction and discussion and stimulating companionship during the last two years. The present work is essentially identical with a thesis entitled 'The Political Organization of Swat Pathans' submitted there as a Ph.D. thesis.

Cambridge, 1957   F. B.

Contents

'As Mahmoud of Ghazni's troops were returning from the conquest of Swat, his wife met the army in Swegalei Pass [by Nikbi Khel]. She inquired about her sons, but they answered evasively. Finally they told her that her sons were dead. The mother then cursed the new land, saying it should be called Ghowgha [*lit.*: commotion, anarchy], and may it always remain unsettled and in chaos; and so it has been up till this day.'

(*from a traditional account of the conquest of Swat by Mahmoud of Ghazni, c.* A.D 1000)

I

Introduction

THE MAIN PURPOSE of the present study is to give a descriptive analysis of the political system of Swat, with special reference to the sources of political authority, and the form of organization within which this authority is exercised. Political systems have been described as the systems for the 'maintenance or establishment of social order, within a territorial framework, by the organized exercise of coercive authority through the use, or possibility of use, of physical force' (Radcliffe-Brown in Fortes and Evans-Pritchard, 1940, p. xiv).[1] But physical force, or the threat of it, is in Swat a characteristic sanction in a great many relations; and positions of authority are supported by other sanctions as well as force. Schapera, commenting on Radcliffe-Brown's definition, says: 'In studying political organization . . . we have to study, in fact, the whole system of communal leadership and all the functions (as well as the powers) of the leaders; and in this context such activities as the organization of religious ceremonies or collective hunts, or the concentration and redistribution of wealth, are as relevant as the administration of justice and similarly significant for comparative purposes' (Schapera, 1956, pp. 218-9).

Radcliffe-Brown's definition, moreover, does not apply equally to different levels of Swat Pathan organization. In Swat there are small local groups which maintain internal order through coercive authority, supported by physical force. But there are also larger populations characterized by a social order without a clear demarcation of territorial units; and physical sanctions are not applied by any organized body of persons with the purpose of maintaining this order—it is an unsought product of the way in which smaller groups meet in interaction and opposition.

Political systems constructed on this latter pattern have lately received considerable attention, since it is characteristic of the acephalous lineage organizations of many areas (see Fortes, 1953). Though the organization in Swat differs from these, the concepts that have been developed for their analysis turn out to be useful also in the present case.

The analysis of this wider system requires an understanding of the smaller groups with their internal authority system. These groups show considerable structural complexity. A major problem arises from the fact that recruitment to such groups is formally based on free choice. In many

[1] This form of bibliographical reference will be used throughout. All the works cited are listed in the Bibliography, pp. 139-41.

anthropological accounts of tribal peoples, one has the impression that
political allegiance is not a matter of individual choice. Each individual is
born into a particular structural position, and will accordingly give his
political allegiance to a particular group or office-holder. In Swat, persons
find their place in the political order through a series of choices, many of
which are temporary or revocable.

This freedom of choice radically alters the way in which political
institutions function. In systems where no choice is offered, self-interest
and group advantage tend to coincide, since it is only through his own
group that any individual can protect or improve his position. Where, on
the other hand, group commitments may be assumed and shed at will,
self-interest may dictate action which does not bring advantage to the
group; and individuals are able to plan and make choices in terms of
private advantage and a personal political career. In this respect the
political life of Swat resembles that of Western societies. Many of the
politically active individuals in Swat clearly recognize the distinction
between private and group advantage, and when faced with a choice they
tend to consider the former rather than the latter. This is most clearly
demonstrated by the way in which members of any group may secede and
attach themselves to another when this is to their advantage. Thus the
authority system—in terms both of the relations of dominance and submission and of the alignment of persons in groups—is built up and maintained through the exercise of a continual series of individual choices.

This poses some awkward problems in analysis. One might attempt to
analyse the political system in Swat as the sum of all the choices of individuals giving their allegiance to others, describing the alternative
patterns and possibilities which are presented to them, and the bases on
which they make their choices. But these bases of choice are in fact not
available for observation. An essentially similar, but more convenient,
approach reverses the emphasis and analyses the system in terms of the
observable activities of the political leaders. This follows the general lead
of writers such as Weber (1947), who analyses the bases of legitimacy, and
de Jouvenel (1945), who sees political activity in a means-to-end framework as directed towards rallying supporters for desired purposes. In such
a framework, allegiance is regarded not as something which is given to
groups, but as something which is bartered between individuals against a
return in other advantages. The system of authority and the alignment of
persons in groups is thus in a sense built by the leaders through a systematic
series of exchanges. This corresponds closely to the Pathan idea of relations
between super- and sub-ordinates as reciprocal but differentiating contracts. Our central problem then is to explore the kinds of relationship that
are established between persons in Swat, the way in which these may be
systematically manipulated to build up positions of authority, and the variety
of politically corporate groups which result. The advantage of this form
of analysis is that the relevant primary data consist in observable actions.

The distinction drawn by Firth between social structure and social organization may be utilized in this analysis. While the existing organization is the result of a multitude of choices, certain structural features of the society, which I shall here refer to as 'frameworks', serve to define and restrict the alternatives which are offered to each actor.

After a brief ecological and ethnological sketch of the area, I shall successively describe the formal frameworks of the society, the network of kinship and neighbourhood ties, and the dyadic relationships implying some form of dominance and submission between partners. Against this background I shall proceed to show the primary political groups which develop around single leaders, and finally the alignment of these leaders and groups into a larger political system.

The description thus takes the form of a progressive synthesis. The argument, and the material on which it rests, is briefly as follows:

Though the authority-relations of each individual are the product of a series of choices, certain aspects of each individual's position are ascribed to him by birth and residence. Every individual is thereby placed in several formal frameworks, namely a territorial system of areas, sub-areas, villages and wards, and a caste system of roughly ten major, hierarchically ordered hereditary castes. Furthermore, full citizenship is vested only in members of the landowning Pakhtun caste, and these serve as political patrons for all members of the lower castes. The patrilineal descent groups of these Pakhtuns thus offer a third framework for the whole society, since as political clients of members of these descent groups non-members are assigned positions in relation to one another.

Between the constituent households of the society there is a network of kinship and neighbourhood ties, which combine to place each person in a unique position in the web of local relations between villagers. This position is the result of a person's membership in local community associations, and the ties contracted by marriage.

But no position in the above formal frameworks, or local webs of relationships, necessarily implies allegiance to a particular political office-holder, or dominance over any specific other person.[1] All relationships implying dominance are dyadic relationships of a contractual or voluntary nature. The primary elements from which the system of authority is constructed are such dyadic relations. These elements of authority emerge clearly in the daily life of Pathans—they are conceptualized by the actors themselves. Thus any person can describe in appropriate terms the bonds which define his various relations of dependence on others, and thus his reasons for submitting to the authority of these other persons, or inversely, the sources of his authority over others. The relations which give a position

[1] There is one exception to this statement: A rule in force in one of the thirteen main territories included in this study requires all members of a ward, while maintaining their various mutual commitments, to give allegiance to the chief who at any given time is dominant in the ward (see Chapter 7).

of dominance and authority to one partner are occupational contracts, house tenancy contracts, membership of men's houses and religious tutelage.

Political action, in this setting, is the art of manipulating these various dyadic relations so as to create effective and viable bodies of supporters— in other words, so as to create corporate political followings. Both Pakhtun landowners and persons of holy descent are active as political pretenders; thus two different types of primary political group emerge, namely the Pakhtun chief with his following, and the Saint with his following.

Finally, such primary groups combine to form the wider political system, which has the form of two large, dispersed, internally co-ordinated alliances or blocs. The form of these blocs may be understood as the result of regularities in the activities and choices of their constituent individual leaders. Such regularities may be seen to reflect structural tensions implicit in the formal framework of the society, mainly those between collaterals in the Pakhtun descent organization. The political system of Swat thus does not define a set of formal structural positions—it emerges as a result of individual choices. But these choices represent the attempts of individuals to solve their own problems; and as some of these problems spring from features of the formal organization, the form of the political system may, through this method of analysis, be seen in part to reflect such features.

2

General Ecology and Ethnology of Swat

ECOLOGY

THE PASHTO-SPEAKING PEOPLE of the Swat valley belong to a group loosely called Yusufzai Pathans or Afghans. This category includes all the descendants of a common distant ancestor, Yusuf, and those persons who are politically dependent on them. The Yusufzai number about one million, and occupy parts of the administered district of Peshawar and the valleys of the Panjkora and Swat rivers in tribal territory. The population in the Swat valley approximates 400,000.[1]

The Swat valley is delimited by natural boundaries. The Swat river arises among high mountains of 18,000 to 19,000 ft.—a geographical extension of the main Himalayan chain to the west of the Indus—and flows southward. Passes at an altitude of 12,000 to 16,000 ft. lead from the upper Swat valley to the Panjkora valley in the west, the Gilgit depression in the north, and the Indus river gorge in the east. In its lower course, the valley widens, descending below 3,000 ft., and bends progressively westward, but is still flanked by high (6,000 to 10,000 ft.) barren mountains which effectively close it in. Finally, the river enters a narrow defile and breaks southward through the mountain barrier into the Peshawar plain, where by several meandering courses the water joins the Kabul river. The valley, from its point of origin to the defile, is about 120 miles long, and for all practical purposes closed off by mountains on all sides.

Communications do not follow the river through the defile, but pass over the surrounding mountains. Contacts with Buner and Peshawar are mostly over the Malakand, Shahkot, Mora or Karakar Passes. Only one trade route, of minor importance, passes through the area: that from Nowshera across the Swat River at Chakdarra, over a low pass and into the Panjkora valley, giving access via the Lowari Pass (10,000 ft.) to Chitral and central Asia. Thus the Swat valley is a dead end as far as communications are concerned. Its historical isolation from any part in the ancient and extensive trade connexions centering in Peshawar is best illustrated by the fact that tea, as a commodity of general use, only arrived in the area some thirty to forty years ago, and has still not penetrated to the highest part of the valley.

Climate is very much a function of altitude. Summer temperatures in

[1] This figure is only a crude estimate, as there has never been a census of the area in question.

the valley bottom reach 105°F; in winter there may be brief periods of frost, with sleet and snow. In the higher parts of the valley a certain amount of snow accumulates through the winter. There are two wet seasons; the winter rains, with some snow, fall between December and March and the summer monsoon season is in July and August. The total yearly precipitation is about thirty inches.

The natural vegetation of the lower valley is dry bush; the areas surrounding shrines are inviolate, and usually have an open cover of stunted, thorny trees or sage bush. Pine forests appear above about 5,000 ft.

The Pathan population supports itself by the intensive cultivation of grain, which is highly developed. This is supplemented by some cattle breeding, particularly for dairy products and manure. For a purely agricultural and herding population, settlement is extremely dense; it can be roughly estimated at eight hundred persons per square mile of productive land. Even today trade is only limited, and there are no cash crops apart from the recent development of orange orchards in a few villages, notably Thana. Traditionally, the economy functioned entirely without money or other currency. In the outlying areas, money is still rarely seen.

In the Swat valley bottom two crops can be raised in a year, the first harvest falling in May-June, the second in October. The total yield of the main crops for the whole of Swat State (population 550,000) was, according to the 1953 tax estimates: maize 160 mill. lb., wheat 56 mill. lb., rice 36 mill. lb., barley 24 mill. lb. (Zabeeh, 1954, p. 18). In the Swat valley proper the proportion of rice in the total is considerably higher. In addition, mustard, sugar-cane, lentils, and a great variety of fruits and vegetables are grown in considerable quantities.

Agricultural land falls into four main categories: *lálma/bārāni*—unirrigated; *qás*—artificially irrigated; *shōrgára*—naturally irrigated, swamp; *bāgh*—irrigated garden. Water is drawn from the main Swat river and from its smaller tributaries by a complex system of channels, which irrigate a large part of the valley bottom. Only irrigated land can produce a second crop of any significance.

Wheat, barley and mustard are grown in the spring, mainly on unirrigated land which depends on late winter rains and accumulated moisture from the winter season. At this time of year the fields close to the river which are too moist for wheat, are used for clover for animal fodder, and as nursery beds for rice. For the second crop the largest possible area is irrigated. Here transplanted rice and also maize are grown. The higher, unirrigated fields are now left fallow, or else utilized for small quantities of crops such as maize. Fruit and vegetable gardens are cultivated separately, and systematically irrigated in the manner appropriate to the particular crop.

The fertility of the land is maintained by manure from the domesticated animals, which is allowed to decompose, mixed with some vegetable matter, in deep compost pits, before it is spread through the fields. Unirrigated land is sometimes left fallow in a two- or three-year cycle. There is some attempt to organize a rotation of maize and rice crops, but as there are no good alternative food crops the possibilities of this are limited. The fields are ploughed and cross-ploughed with a simple plough, drawn by bullocks, which is crudely constructed by the local carpenter and blacksmith; it does not turn the earth effectively and cannot cut sod.

The main domesticated animals are bullocks for agricultural work, cows and particularly water buffalo for milk and meat, sheep and some goats for meat and wool, fowls for eggs and meat, and donkeys, mules and horses for transportation.

The important points to bear in mind in the present context are the high density of population, the diversity and complexity of crops and productive techniques, the very high productivity of the land which is carefully maintained, and its high value, which is the result of the above factors, and of the considerable capital investment in irrigation works which is necessary to maintain this level of production.

HISTORY

The Pashto-speaking population of Swat takes its name from the *Yusufzai* tribes which at present dominate the area. This dominance was established between A.D. 1500 and 1600, when the Yusufzai, driven out of the Kabul valley, entered the northern Peshawar plain as conquerors and progressively wrested control of the Swat valley from the Swati tribe (Plowden, 1875). Some Swati became subject to the invaders; others fled eastward across the Indus, where one can find their descendants today established as conquerors and landowners in the Hazara dist'ict. The Yusufzai invasion was the last of a series of waves of migration and conquests by Pashto-speaking groups which emanated from the mountains to the north-west and flowed into the Peshawar area and towards Panjab, extending incidentally into the Swat valley. The Swati, whom the Yusufzai replaced, had themselves arrived in the area only some two hundred years before in pursuit of the vanquished Dilazak. Before them again the Swat valley had been conquered by Mahmud of Ghazni (c. A.D. 1000), who is prominent in Pathan tradition as having first converted the people to Islam. Though it was probably Hindu at the time of Mahmud of Ghazni's invasion, in the earlier centuries of the Christian era, Swat was a fairly prominent centre of Buddhism, and was visited as late as A.D. 752 by the Chinese Buddhist *Wu Kong* (Stein, 1929). Extensive architectural ruins, and finds of Bactrian coins and sculpture in the Gandhara style, indicate the importance and sophistication of Buddhist Swat; some exploratory work in these historical questions has been done by Sir Aurel Stein (1929, 1930).

In spite of these recurrent invasions, there are still populations in the uppermost section of the valley who are non-Pathan, and entirely alien in language and culture to the occupants of the rest of the territory. Though they speak two distinct languages, they are generally lumped with other mountain people under the name Kohistani. They have a tradition that they formerly occupied the more fertile areas to the south, and have been identified with at least a section of the old Buddhist population (Stein, 1929). The Kohistani languages belong to the Dardic language family (Barth & Morgenstierne, 1956) and are thus related to those of Gilgit and Kashmir. Kohistani settlements are found only where the valley bottom lies above 5000 ft.; this is the altitude above which it is impossible to raise two cereal crops a year. It seems reasonable to relate the upward limits of Pathan expansion to this ecological limiting factor (Barth, 1956).

THE PRESENT SITUATION

The official political status of the area has consequences for the form which political activity takes among Swat Pathans. The Swat valley lies wholly in tribal territory, i.e. in an area which formally had complete local autonomy. The political and strategic implications of this arrangement for British India have been much discussed for several generations (see e.g. Bruce, 1900). 'Local autonomy' as interpreted in Swat allowed the indigenous population complete freedom to work out their own political problems in any manner they chose. Not only did the Indian Government refrain from interference; it also protected the tribes from other external interference, particularly from the dynastic centre in Afghanistan. It is thus possible to an extent which is very unusual to analyse political developments purely in terms of internal factors. This statutory autonomy has been modified in two ways only. The Malakand Agency was established in 1895, in order to protect British strategic interests in a road for pack transport which leads to the administered territory of Chitral by way of the lower Swat valley and Dir. The lower end of the valley (about one third of its area) was included in the Agency; recognized chiefs were paid annual subsidies for their part in observing the treaty relating to traffic on the road, and a political officer in Malakand was made available to serve as mediator in the case of conflicts between them.

Later a centralized state developed in the remaining part of the Swat valley which gradually replaced, or overlaid the original anarchical system. In 1926 the ruler of this State, who had established his control down to the limits of the Malakand Agency, was officially recognised by the Indian Government and given a yearly allowance. The Ruler of Swat State thus achieved a status similar to that of other Indian Princes in treaty relations with the Government of India. Administrative interference, however, was still kept to the minimum.

Since the partition of British India—when both the Malakand Agency and Swat State enthusiastically joined Pakistan—relations with central and provincial governments have become progressively closer, but at the time of my fieldwork no radical changes in administrative policy had been introduced. Thus actual conditions approximate closely to the ideal of local autonomy. In the lower part of the valley, the locally autonomous administration operates in a relatively unmodified and uncentralized tribal system. In Swat State, the recently developed central administration wields power, but to a very considerable extent continues to depend on the tribal institutions for the maintenance of its authority and execution of its decisions. Since this fieldwork was completed, the area has been included *de jure*, but as yet not *de facto* in the province of West Pakistan.

VILLAGE ORGANIZATION

Village organization, and political life in general, are profoundly influenced by two complexes of myths and values common to the whole Swat area. One of these relates to land tenure and the status of the 'landed gentry', the other to religious ascendancy and its relevance to daily life.

According to the first, the Yusufzai tribes entered the valley as conquerors; their descendants claim ownership and jurisdiction over all land, with exceptions to be noted later. Tradition tells how the conquering Yusufzai had great difficulty in arranging an equitable division of the spoils of conquest; they appealed to a prominent holy man, Shaikh Malli, to do this for them; and he devised a system which was at the same time both completely just and permanent.[1] He saw that the members of the group were all sons of Yusuf, but subdivided into branches according to the degrees of collateral distance between them, i.e. in terms of their relations to each other through their closer patrilineal ancestors. He divided the valley into regions, corresponding to the number of sub-tribes (i.e. major divisions of the tribe), and allotted one to each. In his further subdivisions Shaikh Malli took note of the particular pattern of subdivision of the sub-tribe to which any region had been allotted. Where that group had two main branches, he divided the region in two parts; where there were three main branches, he divided the region in three parts. In other words, he delimited a hierarchy of territorial segments corresponding to the particular pattern of segmentation within the major Yusufzai lineages. But no two pieces of land are really equal. So rather than vest property rights to specific fields permanently in any one lineage segment, Shaikh Malli decreed that the land should be periodically re-allotted. Where the sub-tribe had two main branches, these two should alternate, say every ten years in their occupation of the two halves of the region. Thus after twenty years both branches would have occupied both areas equally long. Where there were three main branches, the sub-regions were passed round in a circle, so as to give a thirty-year cycle. In this system, individuals do not own land in the sense of having rights to particular fields; they hold shares in the total landed assets of the sub-tribe. In this way, a completely equitable division of the fruits of conquest was assured. Since the areas thus periodi-

---

[1] This tradition is substantiated by the reported existence of a manuscript, written by Shaikh Malli himself, describing the Yusufzai conquest of Swat and his own part in measuring and allotting the conquered areas (see Raverty, 1860, p. 32).

cally re-allotted were large, this arrangement involved a wholesale migration of landowners over distances of thirty miles or so every ten years.
The non-Yusufzai majority of the population never took part in these
moves. The land tenure system thus emphasized the division between
landowning Yusufzai conquerors and their subjects, the former being a
dominant, cosmopolitan 'gentry', the latter a parochial, subordinate
population, serving a succession of different lords.

This division is further emphasized by restrictions on intermarriage
which lead to the development of social groups of a caste type. Pathans
allow the marriage of equals, even when close relatives, and the giving of a
daughter to a man of superior status, but discourage the giving of women
in marriage to inferior men. Landowners, as a group, thus tend to marry
endogamously, but they also take some women in marriage from lower
groups, whereas they will not give their daughters in marriage to inferiors.

In occupation the two groups stand in a symbiotic relationship. The
landowners are ideally warriors and administrators, the wealthier among
them delegating all agricultural work to tenants. Men with small holdings
do frequently work their own land, but are prevented by their ideals of
pride and independence from becoming the tenants of others. Non-landowners follow very diverse occupations. The main categories are tenant
farmers, labourers, blacksmiths, carpenters and other craftsmen, muleteers,
shopkeepers, barbers, and shepherds. All alike are directly or indirectly
dependent on the landowners both politically and economically.

In the second place, Swat Pathans subscribe to the Moslem religion and
recognise the moral virtues which it inculcates.[1] In terms of these virtues,
a variety of statuses depend on sanctity, piety, religious learning, or
dedication. Such statuses are generally regarded in Swat as inheritable,
and numerous descent groups claim authority and high rank by virtue of
their descent from the Prophet Mohammed, or from saints, scholars or
devotees. The validity of these claims, though based on fundamentally
different criteria from those of the Yusufzai landlords, is admitted by all,
and persons of such 'holy' status occupy a special position in society. They
are generally described in English, pace Islamic theology, as 'Saints'. The
role of Shaikh Malli, as sketched above, in devising a just settlement
between groups with conflicting interests, may be taken as a typical
example of the political significance of such a position.[2]

The attitudes towards intermarriage of landowners and persons of 'holy'
status illustrate their different views of their relative rank. Some men in
'holy' positions assert that they will marry the daughters of landowners

---

[1] Koran, Surah 49, 14: 'Verily we have created you of male and female. . . .
Verily the most honourable of you in the sight of God is the most pious of you.'
[2] History of Swat, p. 10: 'Saints and Sayyids have been mainly responsible for
the maintenance of peace and quietude and other beneficial measures for the settlement of the country and its people . . . even in our own time peace is maintained by
these worthy mystics in places where no settled Government or State exist.'

but not give their own daughters in return, while landowners insist that they intermarry with 'holy' descent groups only on terms of reciprocity.

In return for their services as political mediators, tribal segments of the Yusufzai occasionally grant prominent holy men permanent rights to land. Such plots are then withdrawn from re-allotment, and the area of the traditional 'shares' is slightly reduced in the territory of the sub-tribe. In such manner, and by the conquest of marginal land from non-Yusufzai groups such as the Kohistani tribes in the upper valley, descent groups with 'holy' status often emerge as landowning groups of a different type from the Yusufzai landowners. Occasionally 'holy' leaders may even become independent political rulers. In all cases they claim some political or adminstrative authority, and take an active and at times prominent part in political life.

A village—or the basic unit of government, a ward of a village—is thus inhabited by a diverse group of persons. Each ward is usually led by a single chief, who must be a Yusufzai landowner and is confirmed in his position by all landowners of the ward. Such a chief has a variety of relationships with different categories of his subjects: his fellow landowners who are his lineage equals and potential rivals; his own tenants and dependants; the tenants and dependents of other landowners; 'holy' men; and the tenants, dependents and religious followers of the 'holy' men. Relations with persons outside the ward are equally complex. The fear is prominent in the mind of every Pathan chief, that his nominally subject lineage mates, and persons of holy status, are intriguing behind his back with outsiders, just as he himself is intriguing with the nominal followers of other chiefs.

The political activities of the chief, designed to maintain or enhance his position, centre in the very important Pathan institution of the men's house. In each ward there is at least one men's house, dominated by a chief; and the political, economic and recreational life of the men of the ward revolves around this common centre. Allegiance to the chief is expressed by the mere act of visiting his men's house. This allegiance is reinforced and deepened by the acceptance of hospitability from the chief. The chief is continually giving food, and occasionally other valuables, and thus creating debts and dependence on the part of the persons who sit in his men's house.

Thanks to the great productivity of the land, chiefs and other landowners are able to collect large quantities of grain from tenants—from three quarters to four fifths of the gross crop. Such masses of grain far exceed the household needs of the chief, but in the local non-monetary system they cannot be converted into imperishable capital. If not consumed by others, a great deal of this grain would simply rot. Yet the hospitality of the chief is much more than the mere giving away of his excess wealth. Under the pressure of strong competition, Pathan chiefs intensify their spending far beyond what they have gained from their land, till they have either consolidated their positions by a temporary reduction in their property, or else lost their position and wasted all their property in the process. Many observers have noticed how precious is political status among Pathans and Afghans.[1] This striking hospitality and reckless spending only seems intelligible if we recognize that the underlying motives are political rather than economic. It is a development in some ways analogous to the 'potlatch' institutions of many primitive, non-monetary societies.

The essence of a landowner's position is security of tenure. In an acephalous and anarchic system like that of Swat Pathans, such security is only relative, and depends on the owner's actual ability to defend his rights by rallying supporters and followers whenever they are questioned. The chief's reckless spending, giving and hospitality, are a means by which he builds up such a following. The many persons within the ward with whom a chief has social relations are not, *ipso facto*, his political supporters. His lineage mates who confirmed his succession to office, his tenant who pays him his four-fifths share of the crop, his blacksmith who serves the ward in return for a stipulated fraction of the agricultural produce of its lands—are under no obligation to support the chief in other spheres of activity. Only through his hospitality, through the device of gift-giving, does he create the wider obligations and dependence which he can then draw upon in the form of personal political support—in the final resort, military support. The activities of the chief in the men's house thus serve to charge essentially non-political relations with political inequality, as between a leader and his followers.

[1] Ferrier, 1858, p. 304: 'He who possesses a little money and can scatter it amongst the crowd will soon have a sufficient number of partizans to assist in raising him to power. . . . Afghanistan is the country where a man's position is most uncertain: sardar today, tomorrow despoiled.' *History of Swat*, p. 47: 'Every Khan spent thousands of Rupees to extend his sphere of influence so that by virtue of majority of his partisans and followers he should have a greater quarter and more extensive land. After the division [i.e. after the re-allotment of land] the people who went over to the party of a Malik were bound to live under such a Khan, Malik or Mu'tabir, willingly or unwillingly, till the end of the settlement. However much he oppressed them, occupied fine lands and houses, realized from his people the pay of his attendants, barbers, scribes or keepers, took forced labour from them and realized several-fold the money he actually spent, but these people could not raise their voice against him.'

3
Underlying Frameworks of Organization

THE POLITICAL CHOICES of Swat Pathans are not made in a vacuum—
there are several frameworks of organization which serve to order the
population into categories and groups, and which to some extent deter-
mine their political choices. These frameworks relate mainly to territory,
stratification and descent, and will be described successively.

THE SPATIAL FRAMEWORK

The whole of Swat is divided into a hierarchy of subdivisions, all with a
mixed reference both to a geographical area *per se* and to the social group
inhabiting it. Each major region is occupied and owned by what may be
loosely called a sub-tribe, from which the region takes its name (indicated
by the suffix *-zai*, 'born of', or by the hyphenated term *khel*, 'lineage' or
'tribe'). The thirteen regions within the area which concerns us here are
shown in Map 1. Each region has a population, roughly, of 20,000 to
40,000 inhabitants, and is techically known as a *tapa*—the territory within
which land rights are shared by members of a descent group.

The regions are subdivided into local areas, in everyday usage somewhat
loosely delimited, with names derived from their dominant physical
characteristic (e.g. the valley of—stream), from a dominant village, or
most frequently from a hyphenation of two major village names of the area.
All these wider territorial units—the Swat valley, its regions, and their
local areas—may be referred to loosely by the inhabitants as *watan*—a
general term for 'homeland'.

Each local area again is composed of a number of villages (*kɔli*); the
village is a compact group of dwelling houses, associated with a surrounding area of land delimited by clearly defined borders. Contemporary
villages often occupy ancient habitation sites, and many of them have
names composed of non-Pashto word roots (e.g. Manglawar, Odigram).
Villages vary greatly in size, numbering from 500 to 10,000 inhabitants.
The village is the most important unit of territorial reference for a Swat
Pathan, and its occupants are the main focus of his loyalties.

In government, however, the village rarely constitutes a primary unit,
a fourth level of segmentation subdivides villages into wards (*palao/cham/
muhala*), and these wards are the units of administration and political life.
Wards generally contain 200 to 500 inhabitants. Many villages contain only
two wards; in this case they are usually called Upper (*bar*) and Lower

(*kuz*) respectively. Otherwise, a ward may bear the name of its present chief, of the dominant descent segment residing in it, of a distinguished previous occupant, or some other proper name.

The alternative Pashto words for ward carry some distinguishing meanings. Essentially, a *palao* is a ward governed by one dominant, resident Yusufzai chief; a *cham* is a ward governed by a non-Yusufzai,

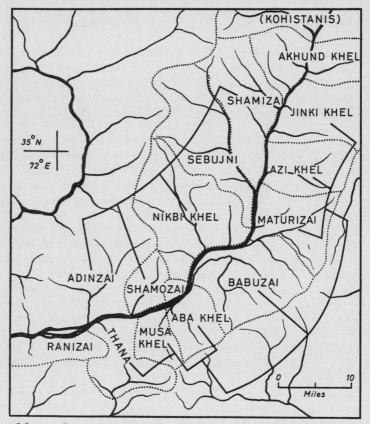

MAP 1. Swat, showing main tribal regions and the genealogical relations of tribal segments.

either a man of holy descent, or a man to whom immediate administrative duties have been delegated by a non-resident landowner. *Muhala* is a more recent Arabic loanword meaning generally ward or quarter.

As well as being units for purposes of government, these spatial units are also made relevant to the constitution of religious congregations. All persons resident in one unit—usually a ward, but sometimes a whole village—depend on a common mosque and a common leader of prayer for ritual purposes. On occasion, even larger spatial groups are regarded as

unitary congregations, as when, during my stay in Mingora, a special
prayer for rain was arranged on the bank of the local stream by a large
congregation from the whole local area.

The local mosque is kept in repair by communal labour, and the leader
of prayer is paid a stipulated amount in kind for his services. In most
villages, there is also some land (*da telo seri*—dedicated land of the oil) to

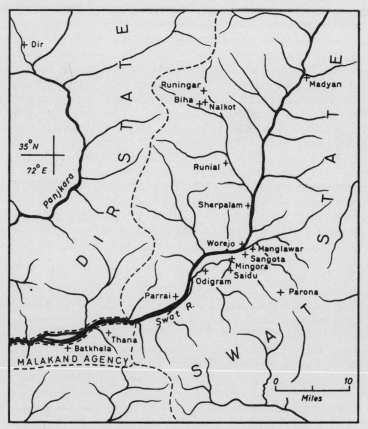

MAP 2. Swat, showing villages mentioned in the text.

be administered by the priest; the products of this land are traded to
procure oil for the lamps of the mosque.

A man's obligations to his local mosque congregation are independent
of the personal contractual relations that he may have with a religious
leader of his own choosing.

Finally, each ward is composed of houses (*kōr*), usually forty to eighty in
number. Each house is occupied by a household, maintaining itself as an

independent economic unit. Its members generally work together and invariably pool their incomes and cook jointly. Every household has a formal head, who must be a male and is almost always the senior man of the group; he has authority over all other members and represents the group vis-à-vis the outside.

Most houses in the villages of Swat are occupied by elementary families, consisting of spouses and their unmarried children, with the frequent addition of persons who would otherwise be alone, such as widowed parents or unmarried siblings of the couple. Upon marriage, a woman moves to her husband, who generally continues to reside with his parents for a time; but within a couple of years the young couple separate from his parents and establish an independent household. The exceptions to this rule are found among landowners, who frequently own large, well-built and often fortified houses, and who depend on their title to land, rather than on their labour, for sustenance. In that class, a son continues to be dependent on his father after his marriage, since his status prevents him from seeking manual labour and his father rarely hands over control of any part of the land. Extended patrilineal families thus tend to develop among landowners, and these generally persist until the death of the common ancestor and consequent division of his estate. Roughly a tenth of the households of a village are of this type.

The distribution of the population on the ground is thus conceptualized in terms of a hierarchy of units with demarcated boundaries—houses, wards, villages, local areas, and regions—and each individual by virtue of his place of residence occupies a defined position within this series of groups.

CASTES

The population is then divided into territorial units with precise boundaries. Similarly, it is also divided into social strata with equally sharp boundaries. Each stratum is territorially dispersed, but hierarchically homogeneous. While positions in the spatial framework are determined by choice of residence, positions in the hierarchical framework are determined by parentage. This hierarchical type of category is usually called qoum—people, religious or ethnic group, caste. The different qoums of Swat constitute patrilineal, hereditary, ranked occupational groups, conceptually endogamous. Each qoum is named, and membership in a qoum is unalterably determined by birth. Sociologically, they might be classified as estates or castes. They differ from castes as usually defined (e.g. Stevenson, 1954) mainly in that they are without ritual or religious importance. But in view of their parallelism and continuity, through similar groups among Moslems in the Indus plain and United Provinces, with castes of the Hindu system, I shall refer to these as castes.[1]

It would be impossible, without a comprehensive census, to make a complete list of all the castes found in the Swat valley. Some of them are

[1] For a more detailed analysis of this system of stratification, see Barth (1959).

associated with highly specialized occupations, and may be found only very locally, represented by no more than a few households in all. The following list is based on a complete census of the four small villages of Sangota, Worejo, Nalkot, and Biha, and on partial censuses of the very large villages of Mingora, Odigram, and Thana (see Map 2). Except for two men of sweeper caste, brought in to the area from Peshawar by sophisticated persons unwilling to wander far off into the bush for purposes of elimination (from villages of more than five thousand inhabitants) this list includes all the castes with which, to my knowledge, I came in contact:

descendant of the Prophet	Sayyid
descendants of Saints various orders of Sainthood	Sahibzāda Mīan Akhundzāda Pirzāda
landholding tribesman	Pakhtún
Priest	Mullah
shopkeeper	Dukandār
muleteer	Pārācha
farmer	Zamidār
goldsmith	Zərger
tailor	Sárkhamār
carpenter	Tarkāṛn
smith	Ínger
potter	Kulāl
oilpresser	Tīlī
cotton-carder	Landāp
butcher	Qasai
leatherworker	Mōchi/chamyār
weaver	Jōla
agricultural labourer	Dehqān
herdsman (in part non- Pashto speaking)	Gújar
ferryman	Jālawān
musician and dancer	Dəm
barber	Nāī
washerman	Dōbi
thong- and sieve-maker and dancer	Shāh khel/kashkōl

Caste in the present context is important because of the way it defines a ranked hierarchy of groups, and the relations between these groups in local communities. The question of the relative ranking of castes in Swat requires some discussion.

To begin with, I should make it clear that I am concerned with secular status and rank—a special system of ritual rank, as elaborated among Hindus, has no meaning in an Islamic framework. This is not to say that there is no notion of pollution; but ritual pollution derives, according to Islam, from physiological or body processes such as elimination, sexual intercourse and death. Thus all men are equally cursed with these sources of pollution, and since purification depends on certain frequently repeated individual and private acts, Islamic notions of pollution cannot readily be applied to distinguish a ritual hierarchy of social groups. There is however a tendency for secular position to be interpreted by Pathans in terms of the polarity pure (*pak*) versus impure (*palit*).

There is thus no ritual occasion or idiom by which all groups are ordered in a linear hierarchy; instead there are several partly independent criteria for the hierarchical position of social groups. Approaching the above list with three main criteria in mind—wealth, political ascendancy and purity —the differences between castes can fairly readily be interpreted in hierarchical terms.

Some occupations are clearly polluting, since they associate the performer specifically with the bodily processes of others, as well as his own. In the case of sweepers this pollution is so strong that the profession as such is repudiated by Pathan society. The status of washermen and barbers, who are concerned with shaving, nailparing and childbirth, are clearly also polluting. So is that of the thong- and sieve-maker, who works extensively with the guts of animals, and that of dancers, since they are associated with prostitution and sin. Apart from the dancers, these 'polluted' groups also belong to the lowest economical stratum, and have no political autonomy. They thus clearly form the bottom rungs on the social ladder. Equally poor, but free from the stigma of pollution, are ferrymen, herdsmen and property-less labourers. These also fall very low in the hierarchy.

The criterion of relative purity produces no further distinction until one reaches the very top of the hierarchy, where belief in the inherited power and superior piety of Sayyids and Saints sets these people apart from ordinary profane individuals. The intervening groups are differentiated by wealth and power alone. Of these the landowning tribesmen, Pakhtuns, serve as political patrons to the others, and are thus clearly superior to everyone but the Saints. Priests do not normally own inherited land, but by serving as Imams they gain access to the dedicated lands of the mosque. Shopkeepers, and to some extent muleteers, tend to amass wealth and are thus placed quite high. Farmers who serve as tenants, as distinct from labourers, are persons of some means. They own cattle, seed and agricultural equipment, though normally not land. They thus have a slight advantage over the craftsmen in that they are more like Pakhtuns, and many of them trace descent from previous waves of conquerors. These distinctions however are of little practical significance.[1]

The disagreements over hierarchical position serve as much as the clear distinctions between strata to emphasize the differences between caste

---

[1] In the accompanying charts I have in fact placed goldsmiths after priests and above farmers, since in the village of the census where they are listed, they constitute a landowning colony of farmers.

groups. Relations between farmers and, say, carpenters are limited, and understanding between them reduced by the fact that neither will recognize the other as a full equal. Thus a complex total picture emerges of multiple ranked occupational castes, each separated from the others by hierarchical differences and other barriers to communication. The conceptualization of these groups by Pathans serves to limit and direct the social relations of their members.

This is most clearly expressed in marriage, where the secular ideal, unsupported by any formal ban on intermarriage, favours marriage between equals but permits women to be given to their social superiors. For a woman's relatives to give her in marriage to a social inferior is regarded as shameful. Figure 1 shows the caste relations between all living spouses in four small villages of Swat. While the high frequency of endogamy is clearly shown, the tendency for women to pass up the social scale does not emerge so clearly. This is partly due to the lack of a clear linear hierarchy of castes, as discussed above. Thus apparent cases of hypergamy reflect the near-equality between for example, farmers and some craftsman castes, or between poor Pakhtuns or priests and rich farmers. The frequency of hypergamy shown in Figure 1 is particularly increased by a series of marriages between men of priest caste and women of Saint (eight cases) and Pakhtun (eleven cases) castes. It should be noted that in one of the communities of the census there is a large group of established, landowning priests, and seventeen of the nineteen marriages are between them and the daughters of fellow landowners of Saint and Pakhtun caste. These marriages can be reinterpreted by the actors as marriages between equals (see p. 37), and the ideology of endogamy with alternative hypergamy is maintained. The tendency to find kin relations concentrated within one's caste is strong enough for the castes to be conceptualized by Pathans as 'families' (sing.: *nasab*).

The castes do not form localised communities. They are primarily hereditary occupational categories, and thus economically dependent on each other, and are necessarily interspersed. As will be shown in a later chapter, the economic organization is essentially the application in practice of the implications of the caste structure. Only where there are discrepancies between the occupational structure required in a local community and its caste composition do discrepancies between inherited caste and actual occupation arise. In such situations occupations not filled by members of the appropriate castes are taken up by individuals of those castes that are too numerous. In Biha village for example, there are a large number of landowners, partly Pakhtuns, partly smiths, cotton-carders, farmers and such, who have managed to secure a small plot of land. These small landowners largely work their own fields, and there is a general excess of members of agricultural castes. Tenant farmers who have been unable to find work appropriate to their caste have therefore taken up various other occupations. Two farmers work as tailors, while others are carpenters and muleteers. But in spite of such discrepancies, the degree of correspondence between caste and occupation is striking. Granting the

marries woman:

man		Saint	Pakhtun	Priest	Goldsmith	Muleteer	Farmer	Craftsman	Labourer	Herdsman	Low-caste
	Saint	25	17	4	0	0	0	0	0	0	0
	Pakhtun	6	90	5	3	7	3	4	5	1	0
	Priest	8	11	28	0	0	5	3	1	4	1
	Goldsmith	2	1	0	9	4	0	0	0	0	0
	Muleteer	0	2	1	1	16	3	4	1	0	1
	Farmer	0	6	7	0	4	42	8	0	10	1
	Craftsman	0	2	1	0	4	9	29	2	6	1
	Labourer	0	0	0	0	0	3	4	13	6	0
	Herder	0	0	0	0	0	2	1	0	17	0
	Low-caste	0	0	2	0	1	2	0	2	1	14

key: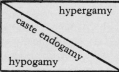
hypergamy
caste endogamy
hypogamy

Total: 476 marriages

FIG. 1. Marriage and caste. Combined figures from Sangota, Worejo, Nalkot and Biha villages. Marriages endogamous to caste: 283 (59·5%). Marriages where women pass up: 110 (23·1%). Marriages where women pass down: 83 (17·4%).

appropriateness of priests engaging in agriculture and trade (their two recognized means of subsistence when holding office as Imam, see p. 47), the percentage of persons engaging in occupations inappropriate to their caste is a mere sixteen per cent in the four villages of the census.

The high degree of correspondence between inherited caste and adult occupation is partly a reflection of the great latitude offered for mobility where caste has no rigid ritual implications. The people of Swat are indeed fully aware that the caste of a family can be changed. One hears statements such as 'they used to be herders, but now they are farmers', or 'they were really Pakhtuns, but ate up all their lands, and now they are smiths'. Such movement or mobility is a slow process. The son of a priest who takes up carpentry will always be regarded as of priestly caste, and so will his son, but beyond that the criteria are not clearly defined: the third generation carpenter might come to be regarded as a carpenter since his father, and his father's father, practised carpentry before him—unless he is continually associated by kinship and locality with his collateral priestly relatives.

In a similar fashion, new castes spring up. A new type of sandal (Psht.: *sapləi*; Panjabi: *chapli*) was developed by a shoemaker in Kohat some forty years ago, and has become the predominant shoe-type for males in Swat. The making of these shoes is an honourable occupation, ranked much higher than common leatherwork, and is pursued in the bazaars of Mingora by persons of a number of castes. It was explained to me that the occupation was so new that it had not yet become the trade of one caste; but no one was in any doubt that it would in time become so, just as tailors emerged as a caste with the introduction of the sewing-machine some seventy to eighty years ago.

The extent of genealogies remembered by members of different castes varies in relation to the actual age of the caste, and to the length of time during which the line has occupied the caste status. The basic craftsman castes—carpenter, blacksmith and potter—all have a core which claims descent from the Prophet David (King David of the Old Testament), who in the manner of a culture hero hammered iron tools for the carpenter, using his knee as anvil, and with these tools fashioned a potter's wheel—thus inventing the techniques, and teaching his descendants the crafts. However, the proof of such descent is patently spurious, and amounts to little more than the mere affirmation of descent from David, passed down from father to son, often even without a supporting pedigree. True, ramifying genealogies are of importance only to *Pakhtuns*, for whom descent traced from the apical ancestor, together with actual land owner-ship, is a necessary criterion for caste membership, and to some extent to Saints, who must be able to document their descent from the Prophet Mohammed, or from some well-known Saint, and who must share the income from ancestral shrines. Except among these two groups, such genealogies as are remembered are not used to support segmentary organizations, but have importance only in proving linear derivation from ancestors in certain statuses, i.e. they function merely as pedigrees.

As will be seen below, only Pakhtuns and Saints maintain any wide-range organisation[1]; the other castes are without corporate unity, even on

---

[1] Farmers who belong to pre-Yusufzai tribal descent groups, and herders who have maintained their ethnic distinctiveness and clan organization, are partial exceptions to this rule.

the village level. There is nothing in Swat to parallel the caste villages and caste panchayats of the Hindu system; all judicial and administrative power is held by persons of Pakhtun or Saint caste. In all cases of conflict (except where close kin are involved) a man identifies himself with such political units, led by Pakhtuns or Saints, and not with caste groups.

By his inherited membership in a caste, every Pathan is for all practical purposes irrevocably placed in a particular structural category within his society. This ascription determines, to a great extent, a person's occupation; it canalizes his marital and affinal relations, it sets effective limits to his ambition and determines the kind of political role he will play in his society. Caste does not, however, define corporate political or juridical units of any kind. Every man is free to choose to which particular groups—whether they be for political, economic, recreational or other purposes—he wishes to belong. Caste membership merely limits the range of positions to which a man can aspire. Caste thus constitutes, along with the territorial framework, another of the premises on which political life is based.

Patrilineal Descent Groups

The character and function of the unilineal descent charters of Pakhtuns and Saints, mentioned above, require elaboration, since these define a third framework of organization. The territorial system lumps persons together in local units, and caste lumps them together in ranked social groups. Unilineal descent, on the other hand, places each Pakhtun and each Saint—and thereby also their political clients—in a unique position in a segmentary system. Though descent groups are not corporate political bodies, membership in them influences political choices. I shall describe briefly their relation to domestic organization, their pattern of recruitment, and their formal structure. Their relation to local groupings will be discussed further in Chapter 6.

Pathans give importance to males and presuppose their authority over females in all situations. As will be seen in the discussion of marriage, this holds true in the domestic sphere as well as in the larger world. Their society might legitimately be called patriarchal. In the family, the husband and father has all authority; he controls the social intercourse of the family members to the extent of being able, at his pleasure, to cut his wife off from all contact with her natal kin; he controls all property; he may use physical compulsion to enforce his authority; and he alone has the right to dissolve the domestic unit or expel its members, by divorce or by disinheriting the children. These are his formal rights. Needless to say, among Pathans as apparently everywhere, people are often unable or unwilling to assert their rights. There are hen-pecked husbands and bullied fathers. Moreover, there are effective checks on the abuse of male authority. Nevertheless, every domestic unit is dominated by its male members, in particular by the senior male. In all relations outside the circle of close kin, the men represent the household; indeed, with respect to rights to make contracts, take decisions, or in any way commit the domestic unit as a whole, they *are* the household. Even women of low status, who are not physically prevented by complete seclusion from establishing relations with outsiders, are still legally prevented from entering into any contract except with the knowledge and approval of their husbands.

Descent among Pathans is reckoned strictly in the male line. A mother has no rights which she could transfer to her children, either in her marital or her natal home; nor does she control any productive resources. She is completely dependent on her husband, and the conjugal pair dispose only of such rights and property as are the husband's, and transmit them, in turn, only to his sons, or, in lieu of sons, to whoever is his closest agnatic male relative.

Patrilineal descent thus receives considerable emphasis among Pathans; adopting the basic distinction made by Linton (1936) between ascribed and achieved status, one might say that patrilineal descent defines the only principle for the ascription of status or rights. But the organization of Pathan society is not exclusively, or even predominantly, based on that principle. Most statuses and rights are usually defined by contractual agreements between persons; that is to say, they are achieved. Beyond determining caste membership, patrilineal descent has its main importance through the relationship that exists between the descent groups of landowners and the territorial organization; this relationship is complex and has undergone profound change in Swat in the last thirty years. It can best be described in connexion with the discussion of land tenure in Chapter 6. I shall here attempt to describe only the formal features of the descent system.

A unilineal descent system is based on the recognition, for culturally defined purposes, of unilineal succession and the equivalence of siblings. These two elements are present among Swat Pathans in the form of an ideology of respect for father and father's father, and solidarity between brothers. Respect for one's father is indicated by name avoidance. A man is ashamed to mention the personal names of his close agnatic ascendants; to do so would be disrespectful to them. In giving genealogies, father and grandfather are given names such as *Malak Baba* (headman old-man), or *Badshah Khan* (king chief). This avoidance is also observed by others, who would often be unwilling even to whisper to me the name of the father of a person who was present in the room. A father's authority is recognized throughout his life; relations between father and son are usually formal, with a tendency to avoidance, and a strong tie of affection and loyalty is always assumed. Relations with a father's father are more light-hearted and intimate, but never such as to derogate from the dignity of the old man, or bring his authority into question.

Mutual trust between brothers is expected. There is some recognition of primogeniture, particularly in the inheritance of formal offices such as headmanship; distinction between *masher* (senior) and *kasher* (junior) brothers is often expressed. However, age distinctions may easily be over-ridden by considerations of competence and personal force. Though each man establishes a separate domestic unit upon marriage, and the inheritance is divided between brothers shortly after the death of the father, full brothers should never oppose one another in public. Opposition between sons of different mothers but the same father is not uncommon, however. Only one case of fratricide was encountered, none of patricide. The fratricide case was regarded as horrifying and tragic. The graves of the two brothers were pointed out to me, but the story was never discussed again.

These moral norms supply the basic ideology necessary for the maintenance of agnatic descent groups. A minority of Swat Pathans conceive of the kinship obligations and kinship terms of reference as extended in classificatory manner to the agnatic descendants of the *lare war-nikə* (distant removed grandfather), that is, within a patrilineage of seven generations' depth, called a *pēṛəi*. This is, however, a pure fiction. Most persons are unaware of the special term *pēṛəi* and its meaning, and there is no attempt to standardize genealogies or the application of kinship terms in this form. The importance of the concept is only in illustrating the ideology in terms of which the domestic relations of respect and solidarity should be extended to agnatic collaterals.

However, since Radcliffe-Brown's paper on patrilineal and matrilineal succession (1936), it has become a commonplace of anthropological theory that corporate unilineal descent groups only emerge in relation to a joint estate, i.e. when the members of the descent unit have a common stake in something. The ideals and norms described above offer the foundations for the development of corporate descent groups; but such groups will in fact only emerge in relation to some kind of joint estate.

The estate over which persons hold such rights in Swat is *land*—the main source of economic and political power in the agrarian feudal society of Swat Pathans. Rights over land, though individual, are held by landowners *qua* members of certain descent groups. Consequently it is the descent groups of the landowners which are of primary concern to us. The common word for a patrilineal descent group is *khel*, and most men, whatever their caste, are able to name a *khel* to which they claim to belong. But the *khels* of non-landowners usually turn out to be no more than names, and the genealogies offered are merely spurious pedigrees. The 'joint estates' of such non-landowning descent units are ephemeral and unimportant: a traditional association with a certain area, giving the members customary option, but no legal rights, as tenants on the land; in the case of descent groups of craftsmen, a traditional monopoly on contracts in a certain area, but no effective means of protecting these rights; or perhaps only a name, and the myth of once, in the distant past of the valley, having been a dominant group of warrior-lords, lending a certain aura to the disinherited group of reputed descendants. Thus I have heard Swati farmers abusing their Yusufzai overlords and cursing the incompetence of their ancestors in the decisive battles of the sixteenth century. Thus, though the ideology is present, actual ramifying descent groups are mostly lacking among non-landowners.

In contrast, they are highly developed among the Pakhtuns. Rights to land and the status of landowner are validated among them by traditions of conquest, and the lineage organization of the Pakhtuns is intimately linked with conquest history. At present, a major section of the Swat valley is controlled by Yusufzai Pakhtuns, the descendants of the Yusufzai armies who left the Kabul valley, entered Peshawar, and were engaged in the conquest of Swat at the time of the Moghul Emperor Babar.

There is much documentary evidence on the phases of this conquest and other tribal movements. Particularly in the period when they dominated Peshawar and the surrounding plain (until the Sikh conquest, 1818-34), the Yusufzai participated in the Persian tradition of historical writing, producing various works, among them Akhund Darweza Baba's *History of the Yusufzai* and Shaikh Malli's description of the conquest and settlement of Swat (these and other sources are cited in Raverty, 1860). The Kalid-i-Afghani of Afzal Khan, with a brief history of the Yusufzai, is available in Plowden (1875). The genealogical information contained in these works, augmented by oral tradition, has been compiled and published in English by Ridgeway (1918) and others. Very few Pathans in Swat have detailed knowledge of these genealogies above the level of Yusuf, but most are aware of the existence of Pashto, Persian and Urdu documents, and of the information contained in English publications. For the upper part of the genealogies, I was usually referred to such sources—these authors had, I was told, made the effort of collecting the facts, and it would be silly of me to waste time doing it all over again.

The existence of this historical tradition, and its associated ideas, has profound effects on the meaning given to genealogical tables in the descent system. In most non-literate societies, unilineal genealogies appear to express the contemporary social distance between groups; indeed, the conscious reorganization of genealogies to fit contemporary social facts has been actually witnessed (Bohannan, 1952: 310). Among Pathans it seems that genealogies have two quite distinct functions. They define a segmentary hierarchy of groups and sub-groups, in the manner characteristic of lineage systems. But they also define a time sequence in a written historical chronicle; they give a relative chronology for migration and conquest history. In the first sense, the genealogy has no finality; it simply offers an idiom for the expression of changing social alignments, and the only criterion of 'correctness' is its fit with social organization. In the second sense, however, there *is* an absolute standard. The events of written history are unalterable; and the correspondence between them and the traditional genealogies in Swat can be maintained by a careful oral tradition, and, even better, possible inaccuracies can be corrected by a careful study of historical

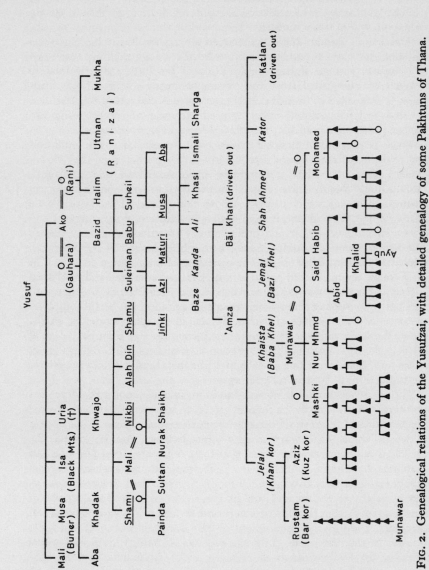

FIG. 2. Genealogical relations of the Yusufzai, with detailed genealogy of some Pakhtuns of Thana.

sources. The repeated statements by informants that I should go to the historical sources, reflect this attitude.

The genealogy of Yusufzai Pakhtuns (Figures 2–4) thus does two different, and at times mutually incompatible, things. It purports to be an actual list of fathers and sons, and it also shows the structural inter-relations of different groups of living men. There is a tradition that nearly ten million Pashto-Afghan-speaking people (excluding the professional castes) are descended from one common ancestor Abdur Rashid, and it is in fact possible to draw up a comprehensive genealogy on the basis of oral and documentary sources. (See Plowden, 1875: 309.) Figure 2 shows the genealogy of the Yusufzai, carried down to the ancestors of the descent groups in the main regions of Swat (whose names are underlined in the figure), and continued to a part of the present generation in the village of Thana, Malakand Agency. Careful collecting of information would undoubtedly have added intervening generations between the names given—one such lacuna in the oral tradition was pointed out between Baze and 'Amza Khan, where the names of one or several links could not be recalled by my group of informants. Apart from the ad-mission of such occasional foreshortening, however, the genealogy is essentially presented as an exact chronological listing of agnatic ancestors.

Though the land tenure system makes the relations between the larger descent groups very stable, some changes and irregularities have occurred, without concomitant changes in the genealogies. Thus, in Thana village, the traditional genealogy does not include all the descent groups owning land. There are seven such groups in Thana, shown in Figure 2 in italics: Khan kor, Bazi khel, Baba khel, Shah Ahmad khel, Kator khel, Kanda khel and Ali khel. Though of unequal strength and different levels of segmentation, these are regarded as being of the same order. An eighth, known as Jambal khel, is not included in the traditional genealogy; it is politically equivalent to the rest but of separate origin as it consists of the descendants of a group of carpenters who some 200 years ago so distin-guished themselves in war that they were given land and Pakhtun status.

The Pakhtun population of Sebujni (see Map 1) is also genealogically compound. Sebujni contains two major segments, Saibat khel and Juna khel; the former is subdivided into Balol, Seina and Shama khels, the latter in Nazer, Zinki and Ranzo khels. Bellew (1864) presents these as descended from the brothers Sibbat and Junah. Though 'structurally' correct, this does not correspond to traditional genealogies, and infor-mants were unable to keep up the pretence of common descent. In the version they regard as 'historically' correct, Juna khel (of Shinwari origin) and Balol khel (from Afghanistan) accompanied the Yusufzai at the time of the conquest of Swat, and together were given the Sebujni area. Later Balol khel invited Shama khel, of Tarkarni origin, and Seina khel, descended from a Saint, to join them, in an attempt to contain the expanding Juna khel.

It is noteworthy that fictitious genealogies have not been adopted to disguise these irregularities. While all other local groups of Pakhtuns have their place in the Yusufzai descent charter, as will be elaborated below, Jambal khel of Thana, and the various groups of the Sebunji, though they exercise full rights as Pakhtuns, do not. The Pathan contention that genealogical assimilation is inconceivable would seem to be borne out, rather than contradicted, by these two exceptional cases.

Our main concern, however is with the smaller subdivisions of these large descent groups, and those which were the actual subject of my field-

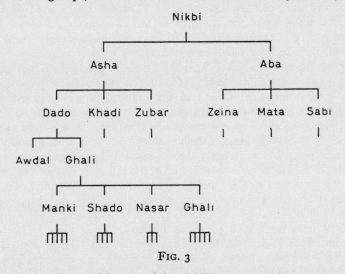

Fig. 3

work must be discussed in greater detail.[1] The pattern of internal segmentation of the group of Pakhtuns of Thana has been given above. Including its dependent villages, Thana has a total of perhaps 20,000 inhabitants, or 5,000 adult males. Of these, less than 500 are Pakhtuns, the rest clients. The area of the Sebujni confederacy has an adult male population of about 7,000 of whom maybe 1,800 are Pakhtuns.

The Nikbi khel is a somewhat larger group, controlling an area with perhaps 40,000 inhabitants, or 10,000 adult males. Of these, some 2,000 men are Pakhtuns and members of the Nikbi khel descent group, the others

[1] The approximate numbers given below are all based on estimates, by informants and by myself. Number of villages and number of houses in villages are based on maps, superficial regional visits, and native estimates. Landlord/tenant proportions are worked out on the basis of a census of one or two villages in each region, and on native estimates. Most numbers given relate to the number of adult males, as these were the numbers given with most confidence by informants, and also of greatest significance for the discussion of the patrilineal framework. In lieu of any available population figures of any kind, other than the official Swat estimate of 550,000 inhabitants in the State as a whole, the following is offered as the only available indication of the order of magnitude of the groups named.

are their political clients. Ghali khel, on the third level of segmentation, numbers less than 200 men, constituting the lineage of the Pakhtuns of five or six villages. The total adult male population of these villages is about 1,000 men. Ghali khel is divided into four segments of twenty to fifty males each. Each of these four groups is further subdivided into numerous family lines, composed of adult brothers and their offspring, and/or adult first cousins, or even on occasion second cousins, and their offspring.

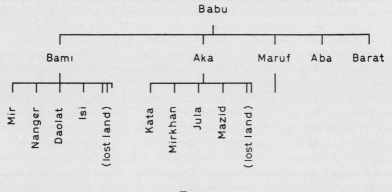

FIG. 4

The most important single group in the history and economy .of the Swat valley is the Babuzai, who control an area with a population of some 50,000 inhabitants. In this area, the proportion of Pakhtuns is appreciably lower, there being altogether only about 1,000 adult male Babuzai. The Aka and Maruf segments have joined, so the primary segmentation of the Babuzai is into four: Bami khel, Aka-Maruf khel, Aba khel, and Barat khel. Structurally, Maruf khel is equivalent to one of the various sub-segments of Aka khel. These subsegments are again divided into component lines of close agnates (adult brothers and full cousins), of variable number in the different sub-segments.

A comprehensive, patrilineal genealogy thus embraces nearly all the Pakhtun families in the Swat valley, and defines a system of groups and sub-groups which places them all in a formal framework. There is no obvious mechanism for the assimilation of strangers into this system. A person's position in it is unequivocally defined by patrilineal descent. But while outsiders cannot be assimilated, the reverse may happen: men born into a descent group of Pakhtun landowners may lose their membership. This happens if they lose their whole share of the joint estate. Membership depends on inherited title to tribal land; and if all the land is lost, the title lapses and the person or patriline in question loses its status as member of the landowning descent group. The process will become clearer in the course of the discussion of land tenure (Chapter 6). It does not, however, modify the formal structure of the descent system. The patrilineal genealogy places every Pakhtun in a fixed position.

It has been remarked that only about one fifth of the population of Swat are Pakhtuns. But the remaining four fifths are also, in a sense, placed in this system. All non-Pakhtuns, except Saints, are allocated as political clients to some Pakhtun. For political purposes they are thereby identified with him and assimilated to his position in the descent charter; when travelling they give the name of his lineage segment as their own 'tribal' name, and for administrative purposes of any kind they are classified with their patron. The descent charter thus serves to organize all Swat Pathans, patrons and clients alike, in a hierarchy of discrete groups and sub-groups.

Only the various types of Saint remain outside the system, and form descent groups of their own. The joint estate of such descent groups is not land, but ancestral shrines, and also the fact of descent itself, which validates their claim to high rank and special privilege. *Sayyids* must produce a pedigree leading through recognized intermediate ancestors to the Prophet's daughter and son-in-law; such pedigrees vary in depth between twenty-five and thirty-five generations. The genealogies which represent the relations between descendants of locally known Saints have a depth of no more than six or eight generations. These genealogies are of significance only to the Saints themselves; to their followers only the pedigree is of importance.

The situations in which the Pakhtun descent groups are mobilized can only be explained after a considerable body of other material has been presented. It should however be emphasized that they do *not* normally form corporate groups for the purpose of political action—for example, larger descent groups have never, in the recent history of Swat, emerged as units in warfare, or in any other exercise of force. Their main importance is in relation to the land re-allotment system, and to the public assemblies for negotiating settlements within local communities.

4

Neighbourhood, Marriage and Affinity

THE PRECEDING CHAPTER has outlined three basic organizational frameworks which serve to order the population of Swat into discrete groups: a
territorial framework, a framework of hereditary castes, and, primarily for
Pakhtuns, a patrilineal descent charter. In a general sense, one may say
that a person's position within each of these frameworks is determined by
the circumstances of his birth. This is true even though geographical and
social mobility, and the possibility of losing descent group rights, give some
fluidity to the system. Each of these frameworks appears to each individual
to. be unchangeable; they define groups or categories which, at any one
time, are mutually exclusive. For purposes of the analysis of political
organization, these three frameworks may be regarded as given and
fixed.

In the present chapter we shall be concerned with another set of
relations—those which are given at the outset of an individual's career,
but may be changed by his own actions. These are the relations of neighbourhood and association, kinship, and marriage. At birth each individual
finds himself placed in a network of established relationships between
neighbours and kinsfolk. But as he participates in community life, he can
by his own actions affect the alignment of persons; his friendships affect
the inter-relations of neighbours, his marriage the kinship alignment. In
Swat these relationships are ordered mainly through local associations for
the celebrations of *rites de passage*, and through the contract of marriage.
Together with the formal frameworks outlined above, these systems of
relations form the background for political activity; but at the same time
they are themselves affected by political events and political designs.

THE *təltole* ASSOCIATIONS

The Moslem religion prescribes certain rites to mark stages in the life
cycle of an individual: notably at birth, circumcision (for males), marriage
and death.

One important aspect of such *rites de passage* is their public nature,
expressed in their joint performance by the members or representatives
of the social groups most concerned. The persons involved in such ceremonial in Swat form constituted corporate associations, known as *təltole*;
the rites themselves are known as *gham-khādi* (sorrow-happiness). In the
following I shall describe the internal composition of these associations,

and the types of activity in which they engage. Their political significance derives from the reciprocal relations between their members.

Essentially, the association is a neighbourhood unit, often made up of all the permanent residents of a *ward*. It is multi-caste in membership, and thus unites persons most of whom are not related by kinship ties of any kind. This corresponds to a strong explicit value: that one should show neighbourliness and a positive interest in the life of all members of one's local community. A distinction is made, though, between the ordinary requirements of etiquette and the stronger community identification with one's association. Thus, a man who settles in a neighbourhood other than that in which he grew up, e.g. through taking employment with a new landowner, will tend to remain a member of the association of his original community. Indeed, association membership is often thought of as being transmitted patrilineally; though strictly speaking the association consists of the households of a person's 'home' community. As an immigrant family progressively come to regard the new neighbourhood as their home, they will assume the responsibilities, and claim the benefits, of full members of its association.

These responsibilities and benefits are practical as well as ritual; members must co-operate in the preparations and attend at the rites performed for fellow members. The scale of the ceremonies is roughly commensurate with the rank and wealth of the household of the person for whom they are held; even so, major ceremonies severely tax the household's resources. The reciprocal support of *taltole* members on such occasions is therefore of the greatest importance.

Birth itself is not much emphasized. The infant emerges as a social person only on the occasion of the haircutting ceremony (*haqīqa*), on the seventh or fortieth day, when he performs his first religious act: the giving of gold-dust, equivalent in weight to his shaved-off hair, as alms to the poor. This event is celebrated by the slaughter[1] of a sheep or goat, providing meat for a feast to which thirty to forty men are invited, most of them as members of the local association.

Circumcision (*sun'nat*—'that which is correct') is attended and celebrated by a great number of people, including all, or representatives of all, the members of the association of the boy's household. The operation is regarded as a necessary prerequisite for men to attain the state of ritual purity required for prayers.

The marriage ceremony is divided into a number of stages. The association is concerned only with the final one, when the bride is transferred from her natal to her marital home. This event calls for spectacular cele-

---

[1] Any slaughter among Moslems is in a sense a sacrifice, as the beast is dedicated to God when killed. The animals used for such ceremonial occasions must further satisfy certain specifications laid down by the Prophet: i.e. be of good health, good sight, not lame, etc. The term *halāl kṛal*, to slaughter, might in this context equally well be translated as 'to sacrifice'.

brations, starting at the bride's home. A festive procession moves to the home and men's house of the groom, where feasting continues for a day or two. All the members of the bride's and groom's associations are expected to attend; those unable to do so must formally beg leave, and name one of the guests as their representative. The members of the groom's association are all expected to contribute food and service.

The funeral is second in scale only to the marriage ceremony. The compulsion on association members to participate in funeral processions is if anything greater than at marriages, and though the emphasis is less on feasting and enjoyment, none the less all these visitors must be provided for by the association of the bereaved.

The associations thus have the practical function of mutual assistance in organizing ceremonies. Whenever outside help is needed for such ceremonies, members of other households in the association assist with both contributions and labour. All members are expected to give such assistance, but strict equivalence is not insisted upon. A prosperous household will consistently contribute more to the ceremonies of a poor one than they will receive from it.

The barber and his wife (see p. 48) are involved in all the above ceremonies; they are, in fact, employees of the association as a whole. The proceedings are directed by them jointly, the barber controlling all outside activities, his wife serving as liaison within the compound, co-ordinating the actions of the secluded women with those of the men. The barber is recompensed for his services by gifts and communal donations on each occasion. Similarly, on the occasions when a mullah is required, he receives gifts on the completion of his duties.

The associations thus have two aspects: they are a formal expression of the participation of all the members of a neighbourhood in the life of any one of their numbers and they are associations for mutual assistance, employing a ritual officer in the person of a barber, and pooling the resources of their members.

In both these aspects, the associations appear to constitute discrete corporate groups. At most times they are so conceived by Pathans. Since most couples reside in the ward of the husband's father, the local association is visualized by every male as consisting of the households of his close agnates and their neighbours. This goes well with the patrilineal ideology of Pathans, and is implied in the common idea that *təltole* membership is inherited patrilineally. But rites of passage are not only the concern of agnates and neighbours. Birth, circumcision, marriage and death are the stuff of the kinship system, the major milestones in domestic life; and cognates and affines, as well as neighbours, are deeply involved in these events. The marriage of a girl gladdens her maternal grandmother, the news of a boy's birth is happy tidings to his father's sister. Relatives of all kinds are expected, not only to take an interest, but actively to participate in the ceremonies both of sorrow and of happiness. The apparently rigid segmentation into neighbourhood associations is thus broken down by the links of kinship, and rites of passage must allow for expression of both kinds of relations. This necessity is usually conceived by Pathans in terms of multiple association membership—a recognized tie of kinship with any person makes you, in one sense, a member of his or her association. Alternatively, the tie may be expressed in dyadic terms—'I share sorrow-happiness with him'—'dē sara gham-khādi kom.'

The range of kin with which different persons share sorrow and happiness varies greatly. Accidental factors, such as the size and distribution of closely related sibling groups or variations in the degree of sociability of different individuals, are important factors in restricting or multiplying the ties between members of different associations. The various connexions of my servant Kashmali may serve as an illustration since, over a period of time, I was able to assure myself of his actual participation in the associations he named. His range may have been slightly greater than the average.

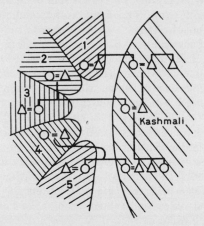

FIG. 5. The associations in which Kashmali participates, by virtue of his cognatic and affinal ties.

Figure 5 shows the five associations with which he and his household are connected, in addition to that of their own local community. Their connexion is to a single household in each, traced through the matrilateral or affinal connexions specified on the chart. As may be seen from the chart, he partakes in celebrations held by the associations of (1) MoBr, (2) WiFa, (3) WiSiHu, (4) SoWiFa, (5) SoWiSiHu. However, he does not take the same part in these as in his own association. He is expected to assist in the preparations for all celebrations by any member of his own association, and to attend them, but in the case of the other five, though he may contribute gifts he has no obligation to keep in the preparations; nor is he expected to attend the ceremonies performed by all the members. Attendance at the rites of passage of members of the households of the particular persons shown on the chart is compulsory. When near relatives of these persons hold celebrations he (and his wife) attend only if expressly invited. The ceremonies of persons entirely unrelated to them, or belonging to different castes, would go unheeded. In the same way all the members of all five associations would not attend the rites of passage of members of his household, but only those specified on the chart, and whoever of their close relatives he chose to invite.

The discrete, local associations are thus connected by a network of ties representing the matrilateral and affinal relationships of all their members. In the preparations for any ceremony only the local association members are mobilized; but at the ceremony itself a larger group congregates, consisting of all the persons linked by intimate ties to the household chiefly concerned. The following relatives of its head are expected to attend; parents' siblings, wife's parents, own and wife's siblings, and married children (especially daughters who move out of the neighbourhood on marriage). Extensions beyond this range are optional, though by no means infrequent. Very intimate ties of friendship usually imply a tie of 'sorrow-happiness', as does a master-servant and patron-client relationship. Non-attendance, without the naming of a representative, by any person with whom such tie is recognized, is regarded as a direct expression of enmity.

The political significance of these associations derives from the relations of reciprocal cooperation between members, and the occasions offered by recurring ceremonies for re-asserting existing bonds. The field of social relations embraced by the ceremonial activities of 'sorrow-happiness' is truly vast. In the course of a series of such celebrations, face-to-face relations are established with distant connexions of *all* members of one's community: the lowliest tenant sees and feasts with the distant affinal relatives of his chief, the chief makes personal contact with the clients of friend and foe alike. Vis-à-vis all these visitors, the corporate unity of the community is emphasized by their joint activity and responsibility for the guests. Vis-à-vis the local community, a person's status and importance in the larger world is expressed by the number, prominence and behaviour of the visitors whom he brings in. And vis-à-vis one's friends and relatives, the ceremonies offer an occasion for the expression of friendly feelings, disapproval or enmity in terms of one's presence or absence.

MARRIAGE AND THE ESTABLISHMENT OF AFFINAL TIES

The importance of marriage in the present context derives from the bond which it establishes between the families of the contracting spouses. An apocryphal dialogue, reported by my servant, illustrates the nature of this bond: Badshah Sahib, the grandson of the Akhund of Swat, decided to become pretender to the position of his illustrious grandfather as leader of all Swat. Jamroz Khan, the great khan of Babuzai, pledged his support. 'Then let this compact be witnessed', said the Badshah; 'give your sister

in marriage to my brother, Shirin Sahib, that we may be allies for ever!'—
This story illustrates the principle according to which marriages are
manipulated in political contexts. But the picture would be incomplete
without mention of the fact that the Badshah and Jamroz Khan later
became opposed. Like most other bonds between persons relations through
marriage constitute only one of many fields of commitment.

Swat Pathans, purporting to follow Islamic law in its Hanafi form,
impose few restrictions on the choice of a spouse. There are no limitations
as regards age. Polygamy is permitted. Incest prohibitions apply only to
the third generation ascendant and descendant, to siblings of father and
father's father, to ascendant or descendant of wife, and to divorced wife of
ascendant or descendant. There is also the prohibition of unlawful conjunction: a man may not have intercourse with, nor marry, two women so
related that if one of them were a male, they could not have intermarried.
Finally, some kinds of divorce create a barrier to re-marriage with the
same woman, without her having first consummated a marriage with
another man. All other women are marriageable. A marriage is legally
concluded by a declaration by the man and the woman's representative,
or the representatives of both, repeated three times before a mullah and
two witnesses. However, certain other considerations have to be taken into
account, notably marriage guardianship, brideprice and the status and
descent of the contracting parties.

Except for the marriages of mature men, not normally their first, all
marriages are arranged by ascendants or collaterals, and not by the marrying
parties themselves. There is legal justification for this in the formal body
of Islamic law: all women, and all men below puberty, have a legal marriage
guardian, without whose consent no marriage may take place. The marriage
guardian further has the right to impose marriage on persons below
puberty. But Swat Pathan practice goes further than the law. The legal
right of persons, on reaching puberty, to repudiate a marriage imposed and
not yet consummated is unknown. Also the power to impose marriage
remains with the marriage guardian throughout the life of a female charge,
and well into the physical adulthood of a male charge.

Marriage guardianship is legally vested in the nearest male agnate of
sound mind above puberty. In actual fact, the power is not unequivocally
vested in persons simply by virtue of their genealogical relationship.
Decisions relating to a person's marriage are made by the whole group of
seniors who have authority over that person; the decisive voice may lie
with the mother, a powerful uncle, or the political patron of the household.
In any case, it is not till a man is the autonomous head of his own household that he is able to choose himself a spouse.

The authority of the marriage guardians, legal or self-appointed, is
enforced by the institution of brideprice. The payment of brideprice is
contrary to Hanafi law: the payments discussed in the Koran are endow-
ments to the bride from the husband and his family—i.e. property which

passes into her hands and will remain with her in the case of a divorce. The bride's father should receive none of this property. These ideals and legal rules have recently been emphasized by theologians and religious reformers of Wahabi and other purist sects, and are particularly attractive to the few young persons who have been affected by Western influences. They have not, however, so far had much effect on common usage.

Brideprice payments are the object of much haggling between families arranging a marriage. They are nowadays specified almost exclusively in Pakistan Rupees, and are also paid partly in cash. The brideprice is divided into three parts:

(a) An endowment in jewellery given by the husband's family to the bride (*mahr*). Though this becomes her property, it is not lost to the husband, since the wife makes him a gift of it after the consummation of the marriage. If as sometimes happens, the jewellery has been borrowed for the occasion, he promptly returns it to the rightful owners. Otherwise, the *mahr* becomes the property of the joint household (*dē ba byā stā kor ta razi*—it will return again to your house).

(b) Expenses for the wedding and equipment of the new home (*wāde dapāra*); mainly foodstuffs, with bedding and kitchen equipment.

(c) Outright payment for the girl (*da jinsi da sár rupai*—money for the girl's head).

The recent drive for the abolition of brideprice has resulted mainly in arrangements whereby a sum representing the last two payments is given ostensibly for wedding celebrations and equipment, on the tacit understanding that a part of it will go into the bride's father's pocket. There is a lowland Moslem custom of requiring a deferred payment to be paid by the husband on divorce or his heirs on his death; this is usually waived after a period when the marriage has proved stable and mutually satisfactory. This custom is sometimes adopted in Swat, as a more sophisticated variant of the practice of borrowed *mahr*.

The payments made on the occasion of the marriage of the servant and tenant of a prominent chief show the relative importance of these items in the case of a brideprice of a total value of £60, which is below the average.

(a) *mahr*: £20 worth of jewellery.

(b) *wade dapara*: 20 lb. clarified butter, 80 lb. rice, 40 lb. flour, 10 chickens, 10 loads firewood, 16 lb. oil for lamps.

(c) *da jinai da sar rupai*: £20.

Large brideprices reach totals of £500, or sometimes even more.

The question of restrictions on marriage imposed by considerations of relative status has been discussed in relation to caste (p. 19). Ideally, a woman should marry a social equal, or superior, and it is shameful to give a woman in marriage to an inferior. Among craftsmen and other specialists such as musicians and barbers, there are added incentives to obtain a wife from the husband's own occupational group—mainly the advantage of having a wife trained in the particular skills required in his own profession, and thus more able to assist him in his work. In all arranged marriages such considerations play a prominent role. Where, for political or other reasons, marriages are contracted between persons of different caste or otherwise disparate status, it is normally the woman who is given to her superior. In the case of such a marriage the woman's family can at best claim equal status with those of her husband: the man's may claim to be superior.

Such then are the restrictions on choice in marriage. In practice a dilemma arises from the inverse correlation between the status of a woman and the brideprice required for her: a well-placed marriage reaffirms a high status position for the family of the husband, but also severely drains its resources. However, these are not the only considerations in choosing a wife. A match may bring purely political advantages. The value of a wife to her husband's family also depends very much on her beauty, her skills and her temperament. Feminine beauty and sexual attraction are very highly valued in themselves. Besides, an ugly woman even of the very best family is a bad match for an ambitious young man; there will be gossip about her looks, his prestige will suffer from having been given a second-rate product, and his relations with his affines will be generally assumed to be. bad.

Apart from the preferences for marriage with a person of equal status, no ideals are expressed, and statistics do not show any particular preference in practice. Once the future spouse has been chosen—through relatives, friends or with the help of the barber—further developments follow their successive stages in a highly formalized course, as follows:

(a) *Kohizdena*, the betrothal ceremony. A formal delegation, headed by the marriage guardian of the boy, proceeds to the girl's village and is entertained in her father's (or guardian's) men's house. The purpose of the visit is guessed, though no settlement has yet been made. To the accompaniment of some ceremonial an agreement may be reached in the course of the evening, in which case a brideprice is stipulated and part payment made, and the marriage formula (*nikə*) is recited by the mullah. The tie is now regarded as unbreakable; legally, in fact, the *nikə* makes the couple man and wife. If the girl dies before the marriage is consummated, her family is expected to find a substitute.

(b) *Khura*, reciprocal visiting, in the course of which the boy goes to see his future parents-in-law, but not his future wife. In the course of these visits his family is expected to make further brideprice payments, and also small gifts of money or cloth at calendrical festivals. These two stages are collectively known as *khparta*—'the movement of feet', i.e. the period of much visiting.

(c) *Prēkund*, the occasion for the final payment of brideprice, apart from the *mahr*, which is given at the wedding, and the arrangement of a date for the latter.

(*d*) *Wāde*, the ceremonial removal of the woman from her natal home to that of her husband. For this occasion she is carried in a palanquin accompanied by a procession displaying all her possessions. Festivities continue for a day or two in the husband's village; but the bride is carried direct to the compound of the groom's family, where she is blessed and kept secluded.

If, as is usually the case, the couple are both sexually mature, the *nikə* ceremony is repeated, in case the boy, unwittingly or as an oath or curse, should have divorced his wife since the betrothal ceremony. By Moslem law, most kinds of divorce create a legal ban on re-marriage with the same woman—however, as the 'marriage' solemnized at the betrothal ceremony has not yet been consummated, this question does not arise. If one or both spouses are still children, the *nikə* is postponed till such time as the parents of the boy permit consummation.

The husband is usually too shy to take part in the wedding celebrations; he hides in the house of a good friend, or in the bush. He does not return to his home until the third night, after the guests have left and the *nikə* has been repeated. When he appears, an elderly female relative of his, preferably a father's sister, prepares the marital bed, and refuses to leave the room till she has been given a couple of rupees.

On marriage a woman becomes part of her husband's group, and authority over her is transferred from her father (or guardian) to her husband. She may not leave the home without her husband's permission. She retains no legal rights in her natal family, she normally receives no share in inheritance, and she cannot appeal to her father or brothers to protect her against her husband. Her sentimental ties to her parents and siblings are recognized, and a reasonable husband permits her to revisit her natal home—traditionally after a fortnight of married life, and later for family celebrations of various kinds. However, if the husband's relations with his parents-in-law are not friendly, he will not grant his wife such permission. When she dies a wife is usually buried in the section of the village cemetery used by her husband's patriline; but usage in this respect varies in different localities. The return of the woman's body to her natal village is a recognized gesture of deference towards affines and matrilateral relations.

The wider ties established by marriage among Swat Pathans are thus very weak. No person, not even the wife, holds simultaneous rights in the two households related through marriage. The ties are exclusively of a personal and sentimental kind. All persons are expected to be interested in the welfare and life of kinsmen, both matrilateral and affinal, and this interest receives its formal expression in the participation of persons in the activities of the *təltole* associations described above.

The marriage tie itself, on the other hand, is very strong. Divorce, though legally simple for the man, is regarded as very shameful and is in fact extremely rare. Where it does take place, the wife will be suspected of having committed adultery with a man more powerful than her husband, and the latter's prestige will suffer heavily. Since the husband has absolute authority over the wife, to divorce her is to admit defeat, and no advantage is gained other than the simple economic saving from discontinuing her support—at the cost of the loss of her labour. There is thus, in a sense, no reason for divorce among Pathans, and good reasons against it.

The political significance of marriage can be understood against this background. Affinal relations are ideally relations of friendship and support; but the relation of connubium by itself does not create significant bonds of common interest. Among politically dominant groups—Pakhtuns, and Saints in villages dominated by Saints—the intermarriage is a recognized expression of sympathy and alliance; but the strength of the affinal bond is not very highly rated. Rather, affinal ties may be charged with political meaning through the addition of other contractual relationships. The ceremonies of sorrow and joy are occasions—one might almost say excuses —for the expression and strengthening of such political connexions, but do not give rise to them. Pathan chiefs and leaders all have close collateral and affinal relatives with whom they have no social intercourse. As political constellations change they find themselves opposed to these relatives, and *təltole* participation is then simply discontinued. The affinal relationship is therefore preferably established with distant allies in order to strengthen existing ties. In contrast to what is found in some other lineage-based societies in the Middle East (e.g. Barth, 1953), marriages are rarely sought with close agnatic collaterals. Several Pathan chiefs volunteered reasons for this: FaBrDa marriage, they said, is known as a device for preventing conflict between agnatic cousins, but it is never very successful. When good cause for conflict arises, such cousins become estranged, no matter who their wives may be. It is better to use the marriage of daughters and sisters to establish contacts or reaffirm alliances with persons of similar political interests to one's own; then one will be strong in the inevitable conflicts with close agnates. None the less, the higher proportion of close family marriages in the two dominant groups is in part due to such political marriages between agnatic cousins, though a more important cause would seem to be the more severe restrictions of purdah. Since no property is transmitted through women, such marriages do not affect the conservation of property.

The marriages of the lower castes show similar trends, though, as one would expect, there are fewer close family marriages. The proportion of men in the different castes who find wives within and outside the village varies with the number of persons of each caste living in the village. The craftsmen form an apparent exception, but this category in fact contains a number of specialized castes. Thus the figure of seventy per cent for intervillage marriages in villages of about 1,000 inhabitants can be interpreted, not as the reflection of a preference for marriage outside, but as the simple result of the fact that village populations are divided into many castes. A man's field of choice is limited to those women eligible for a member of his caste, and the gross number of unmarried women in the village is irrelevant, as is any idea of village endogamy or exogamy as a principle.

	Nalkot			Biha			Sangota			Worejo			Totals			
	A	B	C	A	B	C	A	B	C	A	B	C	A	B	C	X
Saint	12	2	14	–	1	5	–	–	1	–	1	2	12	4	22	·73
Pakhtun:																
chief	–	–	–	1	–	3	1	–	2	2	–	6	4	–	11	·36
others	1	1	1	–	10	28	1	–	7	1	22	39	3	33	75	·48
Priest	2	1	9	–	3	5	3	4	27	–	1	3	5	9	44	·32
Muleteer	–	1	6	–	–	5	–	5	2	–	1	7	–	7	20	·35
Farmer	3	10	18	–	6	17	1	13	14	–	–	3	4	29	52	·62
Craftsmen & Lowcaste	1	6	12	–	4	20	2	3	18	–	7	14	3	20	64	·36
Herder	1	2	2	–	–	12	1	–	6	–	–	–	2	2	20	·20

33 104 308

30% 70%

FIG. 6. Marriage frequencies: A with close relative, B within village, C outside village.[1] The figures pertain to the wives of male residents. Column X gives the total of columns A and B as a proportion of the total of C.

The significance of marriage for political organization may be summarized briefly. The marriage contract itself transfers authority over a woman from her father to her husband; it does not give the husband, or any member of his domestic group, rights or obligations in respect to the property or the persons of his wife's natal group. Thus, while the marriage tie is strong, affinal ties are very weak. Their political importance derives from sentiments which are appropriate between affines, and which are formalized in their (optional) participation in each other's *rites of passage*.

By taking part in such ceremonies, a man is able to extend his social field, and establish friendly contacts over a wide area. These contacts may be of great political value, and presence at or absence from ceremonies may be a convenient idiom for the public expression of political alignments.

[1] More complete genealogical material would probably result in a transfer of some wives from column B to column A, particularly among the large groups of Pakhtuns in the villages of Biha and Worejo. For a discussion of these figures, see text, pp. 37, 40.

5
Relations of Inequality and Authority

SO FAR, I have described a series of groupings and relationships which are basic to the social organization in Swat, but which do not have any explicit political content or significance. Membership in these groups is determined mainly by various aspects of kinship and residence, and none of them are characterized by any internal differentiations.

The groups that will be described in the present chapter differ from the above in two ways: they are internally differentiated, and recruitment is by contractual agreement with a leader. These characteristics are connected in terms of Pathan ideas of differentiation and dominance. Any differentiation of functions between co-operating persons is regarded by Pathans as implying some degree of dominance. Such relations are conceived by Pathans as dyadic relations between one superordinate and one subordinate person. Even where the relation is apparently specific—e.g. a negotiated contract involving stipulated economic services and payments—it still implies a generalized inequality and dominance of one partner over the other. Thus any differentiation of functions within a group is associated with a differentiation in authority; and internal relations within such groups are conceptualized as a series of individual contracts with a pivotal, dominant leader.

The main groups in Swat which are characterized by this kind of internal structure are: productive units, based on economic contracts; groups based on house tenancy contracts, and having certain administrative functions and serving as labour gangs; recreational groups, based on men's house membership; and religious groups, based on relations of tutelage to a Saint. Each such group is characterized by the presence of a single dominant leader, and membership in each is defined by a dyadic contractual relationship between the leader and each individual member.

I should emphasize that the contracts on which the groups are based are, with a few exceptions specified later, all voluntary. Not only is each individual free to choose his partner in any contract; he is also free to refrain entirely from making any particular kind of contract. In other words, a man may not only choose which men's house he wishes to visit or which religious teacher he desires to follow; he is also free to choose not to belong to any men's house, or to be no one's disciple.

In the case of economic contracts and house tenancy contracts, this argument may appear specious, since a person who has no land of his own is, in practice, forced to enter into a contract of some kind to obtain a house and make a living; but at all events he is free to take any kind of available contract he likes.

The importance of these groups to the present study should thus be evident. Since they are based on free contracts, and membership is not compulsory, they do not offer an all-embracing system which can serve directly as a political organization. But through their constituent contracts they define leaders and relations of dominance and submission, and these relations may be utilized by the leaders as a source of political authority. In the following, I shall attempt to describe these groups in some detail, with particular attention to the different rights and obligations of partners in the different types of contracts on which they are based, and to the direct or implicit political authority of the dominant partners in the contracts.

ECONOMIC CONTRACTS[1]

There is no native money of any kind in the Swat area, and the currency of the administered areas, the Pakistan rupee, though widely used, is not present in the required volume to serve as a medium for most exchanges in the Swat valley. Indeed, in the outlying villages with bad communications, rupee notes are rarely seen; and I was forced to import grain from the more sophisticated districts to barter in the more isolated areas for the necessities of life.

Currency is however unnecessary for the smooth functioning of the highly developed system of division of labour and production in Swat. The units exchanged in the economic system are not goods but services; and the economic activities in the villages are organized in a complex system of interlocking mutual services and/or compensations in kind. This system clearly constitutes a variant of the traditional Hindu Jajmani system (see e.g. Wiser, 1936).

Mutual relations of service and/or compensation are organized through a series of individual contracts, and the economic system is best described in terms of these relations. The more important of them fall into six main categories, to be described in the following order:

(a) land tenancy and agricultural labour contracts,

(b) relations between agriculturalists and specialists who supply tools, transport etc.,

(c) relations between a craftsman and private buyers or consumers,

(d) relations between performers of various personal services and their clientele,

---

[1] In a politically autonomous population which is predominantly illiterate, none of these 'contracts' take the form of written documents; they are in fact not even formally made before witnesses, though where conflicts are brought for settlement to the village council or a mediator, witnesses are usually produced. Unless otherwise stated, 'contract' will in the following refer to any agreement made between two or more partners to co-operate in a specified way within a defined field of activity.

(e) relations between a master and his private servant and, finally,

(f) in Swat State relations between the Ruler and his staff, particularly the Army, to be described in Chapter 9.

Of particular interest in the present context are (a) and (b), since the main productive groups are based on these contracts.

(a) Land is held and leased in a variety of ways. The tenure system which was outlined in Chapter 2 will be discussed later. A very marked concentration of land in relatively few hands is characteristic of nearly all parts of Swat. By far the largest area is held by members of the Pakhtun caste.[1]

Even among Pakhtun landowners land is usually concentrated in a few hands. The majority of Pakhtuns are a sort of yeomanry with only small holdings. Most of the land is thus held by a few persons who do not themselves engage in manual labour; they grant occupation rights for specified or unspecified periods to tenants and serfs, who support themselves on an agreed share of the total crop.

There are four types of contract, the holders of which are termed respectively:

(i) *ijaragar*—'rent-companion', who, for a specified period, pays a rent based on an estimate of the net productivity of the land. He assumes all risks on the crop, is free to organize cultivation and to sub-let at his own discretion. The rent is usually paid in kind.

(ii) *brakha-khor*—'sister-of-the-plot'. This type of tenant supplies seed, tools and draught animals, though usually not manure, and in return receives an agreed share of the crop. The share varies somewhat between localities in relation to the average productivity of the land; in the hilly areas such *tenants*, as I shall call this group, receive three fifths (Parona) to a third (Nalkot); on fertile land the usual share is a quarter (Biha, Worejo, Babuzai). Shares are invariably paid in kind. The tenant may be expelled from the land at the owner's convenience as soon as the harvest is finished. There are traditional rules defining the rights of entry of the succeeding tenant before the crop has been harvested, such as his right to seed clover in the ripening rice fields.

(iii) *dehqan*—agricultural labourer, who is supplied by the landowner with a plot of land, tools, seed and animals. In return for his efforts, the labourer receives a fifth of the gross crop. Like the tenant, he can acquire no rights in the land, no matter how long the landowner may have chosen to assign the same plot to him.

---

[1] My only complete figures are from the Barat khel branch of the Babuzai, occupying the land adjoining about five miles of the Swat river, and stretching eastward from the river bank to the mountain ridge. In this area, the non-Pakhtun landowners are predominantly *Lalas* of high Saintly status, and control an area estimated to correspond to twenty shares, against the 160 shares of the local Pakhtuns. This appears on the basis of rough estimates from other areas to be a fairly representative situation for most of the main valley. The proportion of land held by Saints in the hilly districts is much higher.

(iv) *faqir*. This word is a wider term for dependant, but has the specific meaning of a poor man who works on the infertile, unirrigated marginal land of a landowner, and pays for this right in labour, or occasionally in money or clarified butter. Such a person is often called a 'servant' (*naukar*). These crofters usually occupy separate hamlets or villages in the hills or mountain areas (*sarkali* = villages above or away; *banda* = hill settlement). The occupation rights over particular fields tend to be inherited. The amount of service to be given is rarely stipulated, and depends upon the needs, and the coercive powers, of the landowner. It usually includes the obligation to husk the total maize crop of the landowner.

It should be noted, that tenants and labourers have a recognized right to assistance at the peak seasons of wheat harvest, rice transplantation and rice harvest. At such times the landowner is expected to mobilize all the dependants he controls, or—particularly for rice transplantation—to bring in outsiders and pay them out of his own funds. Such payments are traditionally stipulated in terms of shares of the crop: for harvesting, one fortieth; for shucking the maize cobs (woman's work), one fortieth; for transplanting rice, about one rupee (1 shilling) per day plus meals.

Tenancy and labour contracts for garden plots vary considerably, as the work is more skilled and specialized than that in the grain fields. Tenants working in fruit and vegetable gardens usually get a half or one third of the crop.

(*b*) Agricultural production requires more than land and agricultural labour; a group of subsidiary specialists are necessary to produce tools and keep them in good repair, and to provide for the transportation of the crop. In the solution of these technical problems, the occupational aspects of Swat's caste system are used, and a complex set of relationships develops between the different producers and specialists. A single productive unit comprises as a miminum, *landowner, tenant or labourer, carpenter, blacksmith, rope- and thong-maker* and *muleteer*. In Swat, this productive unit maintains something like what industrial sociologists usually term a 'continuous flow pattern of work'—i.e. relations between any person and his supporting specialists are direct, so that the toolmakers respond directly to the specific requirements of other members of the productive unit. There are no intermediary agents, no shops and no storage of finished goods for eventual use by others. Payment of all members of the unit is also deferred till the whole productive cycle is completed, and is generally an agreed proportion of the total product.

The landowner holds the pivotal position in this system. It is through their contracts with him that the other persons become partners in the productive unit, and it is from him that the ultimate profits or reimbursements flow. In practice, the arrangement is usually as follows:

A craftsman specialist, for example a carpenter, makes a contract with a landowner or a group of landowners by which he commits himself to produce and maintain all implements or parts of implements traditionally made by carpenters which are required to maintain the agricultural production of the fields which his employers own. These fields are actually being farmed by tenants or labourers; it is their specific needs which the carpenter in fact supplies. Thus, when a plough is jammed between big stones and broken—whether it belongs to a tenant or landowner—it is taken to the carpenter and he is required to repair it. A similar contract exists with a smith, a rope- and thong-maker, and a muleteer who is responsible for transporting the crop to the appropriate storehouses. Although these services are not directly reciprocal (except between carpenter and blacksmith), the partners in the unit make no payments of any kind to each other. The tenant does not pay the carpenter to repair his plough, the muleteer claims nothing from the tenant for transporting the seed, and gives nothing to the blacksmith for having the mules shod.

At the completion of harvest and threshing, however, the tenant or labourer calls all partners to the *rashā*, the cleaned and dried grainpile beside the threshing ground out among the fields. In the simplest case, shares in the crop are then allotted under the supervision of the landowner to each in proportion to his traditional claim. The crop is usually laid out in long rows of small heaps of equal size. A special servant of the chief— his *nāser* or estate overseer—then passes along the rows and allots one in every four to the tenant, one in every twenty to the muleteer, one each in every forty to the smith and the carpenter, and occasional heaps as alms to the poor. The rope- and thong-maker is usually paid by a set amount yearly. Thus, every member of the productive unit receives his share of the gross product, the remainder—the lion's share—going to the landowner.

The manner of payment—except to tenant and labourer—may vary considerably from this type. In Madyan, a group of landowners may allot fields to blacksmiths and carpenters in return for their services. Elsewhere they are paid a specified weight of grain, of the order of 100 to 300 lb., for every pair of bullocks working on the fields they have served (Thana, Nalkot). Not uncommonly, the smith or carpenter is given charge of a water-powered mill—which he must then man and keep in repair—in payment for his general services to the persons using it. He then collects the traditional one-twentieth share of all flour ground in the mill, which compensates him both for his work on the farm tools, and for his work in grinding the flour (Nalkot, Worejo). The muleteer may sometimes receive, instead of a fixed share of the crop, an agreed quantity of grain per load transported (Thana). These various ways of arranging payment are regarded as alternative and essentially equivalent.

(c) Arrangements of this kind usually apply only in the field of agriculture; the relations between professional specialists and private consumers are dyadic and involve direct payment. Thus, if a landowner or a tenant wants a new bed, he pays the carpenter in money or in kind. Wealthy persons may attach some craftsmen—in addition to carpenters, usually potters and tailors—to their household on a yearly basis, the crafts-

man receiving a stipulated weight of grain per annum. This type of arrangement is said to have been more common in the old days; today most such private business is done on a piece-work basis, with bargaining over the price.

(*d*) On the other hand, relations between the performers of various
personal services and their clientele take the form of long-term contracts.
They may concern such specialists as washermen and ferrymen, but invariably include the priest and the barber. There are usually only one
Imam and one barber within convenient reach of any given customer; they
are under a hereditary obligation to perform their traditional services, and
receive in return a yearly payment.

An Imam receives either a land grant for the support of himself and his
family (Thana, Nalkot) or a fixed yearly weight of grain (about 80 lb.) per
bullock pair working for his congregation (Worejo). Thus in either case the
burden of his support falls on the landowners of the group. In return he
leads the congregation in prayer, and preaches on Fridays and other
sacred days. He is also bound, in return for a small consideration, to solemnize the major *rites de passage*: *bāng*, the reciting of the call to prayer into
the ear of every newborn child; *nikə*, the ritual confirming betrothal and
marriage, and *talqīn*, the prayers and recitations of the funeral ceremony.
Like any other specialist, he also gives private services for a suitable
payment. He recites formulae for the cure of specific pains; he writes
amulets for cures or for protection against spirits and fairies; he cures
insanity by extracting the insect in the head which causes it, and also
disturbances caused by the evil eye.

The Imam holds his appointment for life, and the position is regarded
as hereditary in the paternal line. The congregation, however, may reject
a successor whom they consider incompetent; and where the incompetence
is demonstrable and extreme, saintly mediators will confirm their decision.
The position of Imam is, as far as I know, never held by persons of other
than priestly caste; it ranks too low for the descendants of Saints. The
general status of priests—usually referred to by the less distinguished term
mullah—is low, with exceptions to be noted below (p. 61ff); one of the
favourite derogatory jeers of Swat Pathans is 'you wife of a mullah'.

The Imam is normally required to be present in the community at all
times, but he may leave temporarily to negotiate settlements between
warring groups, wherever they may be, or to travel on business, for the
sale or barter of his yearly income, for a certain portion of every year. One
of his assistants or pupils officiates in his absence.

A *barber* is usually employed communally by a group of households.
He and his wife perform a number of traditional services, and receive an
annual payment in grain, which is calculated either on the basis of the
number of persons in the household served, at about 8-12 lb. per person
(Nalkot, Parona, Thana), or on that of the number of pairs of bullocks
employed on its land, at about 160 lb. per pair (Worejo). His duties fall
mainly into two categories: shaving and hair-cutting, and duties connected

with *rites de passage*. These two types of function may in some places be delegated to different individuals (Thana). One male barber shaves the men of the household at a set rate per year, while an unrelated female barber serves the women of the household, and her husband is called in to perform ritual services.

The ritual services of the barber and his wife are as follows:

He announces every birth by drumming, his wife congratulates the mother, and they carry the news to relatives; for this they receive small gifts.

He cuts the child's hair ceremonially on the seventh or fortieth day (depending on its rate of growth) after informing all the relatives; for this he receives six to twenty rupees' worth in gifts. The hair is balanced on scales against gold-dust, which amount of gold is given as alms to the poor.

He performs the circumcision operation, informs relatives of the occasion, helps in the sacrifice of an animal, assists and joins in the feast— all accompanied by incessant drumming. For this he receives five rupees.

He and his wife are usually sent to arrange marriages, and assist in the many stages of negotiation and the reciprocal food-giving which solemnize the contract. They organize the wedding procession and the serving of food at the wedding. After the meal, guests contribute gifts for the barber.

He informs all concerned about deaths, and receives a larger proportion of the alms than other attendants at the funeral.

He makes all necessary announcements of a public kind after calling for attention with his drum.

(e) Finally we must consider the relation between a master (*naek*) and his private servant (*naukar*). To receive from any person a salary or any stipulated payment is to engage as the *servant* of that person; it implies a general subordination to him. The idea of a professional relationship like that between a Western doctor and his patient, in which the recipient of the service has no authority over the giver, is unknown in the traditional system of Swat. Characteristically, Western medical treatment is given only in two free hospitals supported by the Ruler, in the capital of Saidu Sharif; and the high status practitioners of Eastern medicine refuse to receive payments from their patients, but only accept unsolicited gifts.

Similarly, the idea that a particular role confers *limited* authority is unknown in Swat. A craftsman pursuing his trade in the temporary employment of a person is also expected to perform personal services for his employer; he will, if told, fetch a glass of water, or deliver a message. All persons employed by the State of Swat are the 'servants' of the Ruler (*da Badshah naukarān*); chiefs of high status refuse to enter into this type of relationship with anyone, and have therefore remained outside the growing administrative bureaucracy. My own position was a puzzle to many and a concern to my servant: I obviously claimed a politically autonomous status and acted, on occasion, as the equal of local chiefs; then why should I submit to the dishonour of being the servant of the King of Norway by receiving a salary from his University?

Anyone in Swat who receives an agreed remuneration has renounced his autonomy; he is acting at the command of another person, and is therefore inferior to that person. On the other hand, this frees him from full responsibility for his actions—it is the person who commands who has the responsibility. Thus, for example, if a chief hires a thug to commit a murder, the thug is in danger only while executing the murder. When it is done, all responsibility falls on the chief who paid the thug, and the honour for bravery goes to him as well. Similarly, the recipient of a bribe has renounced his autonomy, and the responsibility for his perjury or deception falls on the giver of the bribe.

The occupation of servant is the only one in Swat that is not associated with a single caste or a limited number of castes; it is regarded as appropriate for all but *Pakhtuns*. A person who employs servants is invariably the owner of considerable land. Servants are of various kinds. The highest rank is that of the estate overseer (*nāzer/kotwāl*), who, unless there are several servants under him, usually has more general household duties as well. The servant is expected to be continuously at the disposal of his master, fetching, delivering, carrying messages, cooking if the master's wives do not, carrying the meal to the men's house, massaging his master when tired, accompanying him everywhere and acting as his bodyguard. The tie between master and servant is usually an extremely close and intimate one—much more so than between brothers, friends, or even father and son—apparently far the closest emotional tie between males that Pathans ever experience. Theirs is a symbiotic relationship: they are unequal and complementary, and the fate and career of the one depends to a very great extent on the actions of the other.

Larger, more prosperous households may also have female servants as nursemaids for the children, or servants for the women of the house. Such female servants often walk about unveiled, and have, as they reach older age, a highly privileged position in the household.

Servants are paid by the year, in kind; usually an agreed weight of grain, occasionally, in the case of overseers, a proportion of the gross crop. As they rarely have large storage-bins of their own, the payment is usually in practice a claim to a share of the grain in the master's storehouse. In addition, they have their meals with or after their master, and receive occasional presents, particularly of clothes. They may also receive financial assistance for such special needs as the marriage of their sons. Sometimes they are in debt to their masters, but the reverse may also be the case. No interest is charged on such debts, and the relationship is usually too personal for the various aspects of debt bondage to become emphasized. As an alternative to a basic wage in grain, servants may be merely supplied with a house in their master's ward, and depend on his gifts for the sustenance of their family.

Finally, slaves (male: *andiwāl*; female: *andiwāla*) fall within the wider category of servants—they are found, though only rarely, in the households of wealthy, politically dominant persons in the Swat valley. They are mostly women, sold from, or arriving as refugees from, Dir and Bajaur. Chiefs may employ them as servants on more exclusive occasions in their men's houses, to add spice to the life of distinguished visitors, though their sexual services are apparently usually monopolized by their owners. Though in fact held captive, and less able than other female servants to resist the advances of their masters, their pattern of daily life does not differ greatly from that of free female servants. Male slaves are very rare; I have no reliable information on their role and position.

Except in the case of slaves, the relation between master and servant is contractual, and terminable at the will of either party.

The economic organization of the villages of Swat is thus very complex. It embraces a series of different kinds of contract, relating not only to land but also to services, between a wide variety of occupational specialists. This specialization derives from the caste system, and economic organization is to a very considerable extent a working out of the practical implications of caste.

Certain features of this system are of great importance for political organization.

As an essentially non-monetary system, it does not permit any considerable capital accumulation in other forms than in land. Rights in land are, however, essentially limited to members of locally dominant lineages of *Pakhtun* caste, and subsidiarily to Saints.

The great majority of economic relationships take the form of tenancy or occupational contracts of relatively long duration, in which payments are deferred or left outstanding in the form of claims on third persons.

In the main productive enterprise, agriculture, the landowner has a pivotal position as the co-ordinator of the many specialists engaged in production, and only through him do the partners in the enterprise receive their final shares in the product.

All such relationships between 'employer' and 'employee'—except for that between master and private servant—are formally purely economic in character and contractually delimited; no wider aspects of political dominance and submission are explicit in them. However, the person who gives the contract is superordinate to the person who sells his skill and labour, and as there is considerable population pressure in the area and far from full employment, the latter is in a weak bargaining position and is in fact eager to obtain and keep such contracts. The threat of discontinuing the contract is thus a strong sanction in the hand of the landowner, and gives him power which he may, if he so chooses, convert to political authority over his contract-holders.

HOUSE TENANCY CONTRACTS

The dwelling houses of the village (*kōṭa*) belong to landowners in numbers proportional to the area of land held by each. Most villagers thus reside in houses belonging to other persons. For this they pay the owner, while, by living on his property, they also become his political subjects, a relationship implied in the terms *faqir* and *kandari*. Thus, while economic relations and land tenancy contracts have no direct political implications, house tenancy contracts stipulate, as well as payments in goods and services, an administrative or political relationship between owner and tenant. These two aspects of house tenancy, the economic and the political, may be described separately.

In return for the right to occupy the house belonging to another person, a tenant must pay a rent (*kálang/kándar*). The nature of this rent depends somewhat on the position of the tenant; it may be in money, kind or labour. Persons not engaged in agriculture (i.e. members of craftsman or service castes) usually have some money income, and often pay a money rent. The majority of house tenants pay in labour or kind, or both. They provide some firewood from the hills—usually about one bundle a month—for the master's household; they are expected, in turn, to run errands for him. They must keep both their own and his house in good repair, and assist—either free of charge, or in return for a small compensation—in his fields in the peak seasons of agricultural activity. They are thus occasionally mobilized as labour gangs in construction work and in the fields. Finally, in most villages, they make regular monthly or yearly payments, usually in clarified butter, to the house-owner.

The house-owner has further rights over his tenants which emphasize the nature of their relationship. On the occasion of the marriage of a tenant's daughter—whether within or outside the community—the tenant gives a standard fee in money and kind to the house-owner (e.g. in Parona: six rupees, two pounds of clarified butter, ten pounds rice, one chicken). This fee, though given by the tenant to the owner, has in fact been expressly supplied by the groom and his father as a part of the brideprice. The house-owner also has the right to a third of any fine collected from his tenant by any judicial institution, from the village council to that of Swat State.

It should be emphasized that the group defined by common relations to a house-owner is rarely a territorially compact group. Pathan landowners usually hold a number of scattered plots of land; similarly, the houses they own may be in several different villages. Within each village, one man's houses are usually concentrated in one ward, but they may be scattered within that ward. Especially where the re-allotment system operates (see pp. 65ff), so that the rights of particular landlords lapse periodically, the tenants who at any one time have obligations to the same landlord form a social group only by virtue of their relationship to him. They emerge as a corporate body only in so far as he is able and willing to mobilize them to joint action. Structurally, these groups are thus like the groups which engage in agricultural production, in that they are formed through a number of individual contracts with a single leader.

The house tenant is under no obligation to enter land tenancy contracts with the owner of the house, but is regarded as having first option on such contracts.

The political obligations of a house tenant are not so readily described. He owes respect, loyalty, support and submission to the judicial authority of the house-owner, in return for justice, security and protection. Neither party to this contract is able, in real life, to live up to these ideals. In a Pathan village, no house-owner can guarantee the security of his tenant; and few practise impartial justice. Equally, the political loyalty of most house tenants is for sale to the highest bidder—in terms of rewards and security—and the judicial authority of the house-owner is often put in question when his tenants appeal to Saints and priests as mediators.

Thus the political content of the relationship will only emerge in the context of the whole set of political claims and counter-claims which constitutes Pathan village organization. The important facts to note here are the ideal of political clientage as a part of the bond between house-owner and tenant, the former's claim to rent from the latter, and the latter's freedom to enter into occupational contracts with masters and partners of his own choosing.

The Men's House

The structure of the men's house (*hujra*) groups is similar to that of those described above, in that each one has a leader, and it is the relations of members to this leader, and not to each other, which define the group.

The men's house is characteristic of the *Pakhtun* caste; it is found only in areas dominated by Pakhtun lineages—which indeed constitute a predominant part of the Swat valley—and not in areas administered by Saints and their descendants. Where it exists the men's house plays a very large part in the daily life of all men; it is at one and the same time club house, dormitory, guest house, and place for ritual and feasting. It is the scene of the greater part of Pathan political life, and is thus of particular importance in the present connexion. However, any description of the men's house in Swat is complicated by the very great variety of types.

Some features of the physical appearance are more or less stereotyped. Usually walls ten to fifteen feet high surround a central open courtyard; rooms form one or two sides of the square, with the roof, supported on elaborately carved pillars, extending forwards to form a veranda. Access is by one, or sometimes two or three carved, stone or metal-studded gates, which can be closed and bolted. The house is thus easily defended. Where it lies on a hill, one of the four outer walls is often dispensed with, so that the rooms and the courtyard face the open side and give a view of the lower valley. It contains at least two rooms, usually three: a large room, with a central fire pit, for communal use in the winter; another for storing beds, pillows, and quilts; and a smaller one reserved for the select and for distinguished visitors, where they may retire and take their meals or their ease. It is furnished with a number of short frame beds, odd assortments of quilts and large gaily coloured pillows, and a few silk bedspreads with fringes, which are supposed to give protection against the large population of bugs and fleas. In the more sophisticated areas the furnishings also include a few European type chairs and small coffee tables.

There is at least one such house in every ward of a Pakhtun-dominated village. In the areas where Pakhtuns form a large proportion of the population, there is rarely more than one in each ward. Where they are in a minority, and each is a large landlord, there tends to be a proliferation of men's houses within each ward, for reasons to be discussed later. But the description which follows will assume that there is only one men's house in a ward. Each men's house is presided over by a chief—the political head of the landowners who frequent it.

Membership of the men's house is limited to adult males. Children of both sexes may enter, but they must keep quiet and out of the way, and are usually chased away if they appear in numbers. Women are prevented by feelings of shame from entering the gate at all, though there is no formal ban; where, in the absence of any males, a female servant is sent, for example to deliver a meal, she stops outside the gate and calls meekly, without showing herself in the doorway, till someone notices her. The men's house is open to all male visitors who choose to enter.

Mere presence in a men's house is no criterion of membership in a permanent social group associated with it. The question arises whether, and if so by what criterion, consociation in a men's house defines persisting social groups. This can only be answered in terms of the allocation of rights and responsibilities. Who can command the building for the holding of ceremonies and feasts? And who contributes to its building and maintenance? No single answer can be given to these questions. The building may be erected and kept in repair by the communal labour of all in the whole ward (Sangota), or by contributions from the landowners among them (Biha), or by the tax income from nomads utilizing the pasture areas of the ward (Odigram), or by the chief only (Thana). Beds, pillows, and such may be supplied by the chief (Sangota, Biha) or by collections from all houses in the ward (Odigram, formerly Biha). Food for guests may be supplied by the chief from his own house (Thana), or by all landowners in turn under the supervision of the chief (Biha), or by the person who brings the visitor (Sangota, Runiyal). And as for commanding the men's house for a feast or ceremony, all such arrangements must have the informal approval of the chief; but unless the plan conflicts with the wishes of other persons whom the chief is more interested in pleasing, he and all others present would certainly applaud the idea of a feast, no matter who was the giver.

So far I have discussed the group associated with the men's house as if it were a corporate group constituted according to some recognized principle and holding joint rights and responsibilities. This, however, is only one aspect of the picture. The other aspect is the position of the chief as the presiding person, and his political ascendancy over the rest of those present. Where chiefs visit each other's men's houses, this explicitly symbolizes a political alliance between them; if one person repeatedly visits the men's house of another, his political subordination to the chief of the house he visits is thereby indicated. 'He sits in my men's house' is a standard phrase to indicate that a person is a political subordinate. In moments of crisis men flock to the men's house of the chief to whom they owe allegiance, merely to sit there for a period, and by their presence there confirm their political loyalties. The eagerness of the chief to encourage all and sundry to sit in the men's house and make use of its facilities, while he bears a considerable part of the expense, is thus readily intelligible. Regardless of their previous relationship to himself, it is in the interests of the chief to bring in such potential supporters.

Yet the men's house—as a club for male companionship, with its facilities for large-scale celebration of personal occasions—is more than a device for the expression or eliciting of political loyalties. It also defines a group of men who share an estate of which they make daily communal use. Membership in a men's house is at once an element in village organization, and an expression of the resultant of all the many elements defining the primary political alignment of persons.

Rarely does one find a men's house entirely empty. All through the day it is occupied by an informal group of changing membership and fluctuating numbers. A married man who spends his leisure time at home with his wife is jeered at. Persons of higher status, with more leisure, spend a relatively greater proportion of their time in the men's house, while labourers and tenants usually do not appear till about sundown.

The morning is the slackest time. At that time work is at its peak, and landowners tend to be out inspecting the work in their fields, hunting in the hills or fishing in the river, or attending to business of all kinds.

A certain number of men return to the men's house before noon, to take their main morning meal there (10 till 12 a.m.). Agricultural workers on the other hand eat their mid-day meal in the fields. After eating and gossiping for a while in the men's house, some people linger on to enjoy the siesta hour there; the chief, unless there are visitors present, usually retires to his home for that purpose. All through the early afternoon sleeping forms are scattered around on beds and squatting in corners, bundled up in their blankets or toga-like wrappers as a protection against flies. Occasionally a man will fuss with the covers, move his bed to catch the breeze or avoid the sun, or fetch a drink of water from the water-jug in a corner of the veranda. A few keep up a murmured conversation. Occasional work, such as tying fish-nets, mending small tools or twining rope, may also be done intermittently through the day.

By 3.30 or 4 p.m. most of the more prominent men, with their hangers-on, assemble for tea—Indian tea, boiled with milk and sugar. After this, some disperse, some stay on, and others arrive; the agricultural workers return from the fields, the craftsmen close their shops. By sundown, most of the normal frequenters of any men's house have assembled in it, some taking their evening meal there, others absenting themselves briefly to eat it at home. Farmers and craftsmen report on their activities and experiences of the day, news of political or economic importance is discussed, and decisions on action for the next day are reached. All through the evening visitors keep dropping in. As the evening passes on, all this interaction assumes a more recreational character; citars and water-pots appear,[1] and the younger men sing, or story-tellers alternate in recounting endless folk-tales. One after another the men planning to sleep in the house bed down, often several to a bed, after quilts and pillows have been allotted to all present. Usually someone has been forgotten; this leads to a re-shuffle and fuss. Activity slowly peters out; maybe one indefatigable story-teller drones on into the small hours.

The extent to which the men's house is used as a male dormitory varies greatly. Unmarried men tend to sleep there more than married men, and men of the Pakhtun caste more than men of other castes. Informants agree that more men used formerly to sleep in the men's house. Its use as a dormitory is consciously related to feelings of sexual shame at being associated with women, and of sons having intimate knowledge of the life of their parents. Such shame is felt most acutely by men of the 'warrior' caste of Pakhtuns, and explains why members of that caste so often sleep in the men's house. Extreme variations are found, from villages where only passing strangers sleep in the men's houses (Mingora) to others where all males do so (Runiyal). The latter situation appears to be characteristic of the whole lower Sebujni area, the most conservative part of the Swat valley. Here all the men sleep in the men's house and only the chief himself goes openly to visit his wives in the evening, while all the rest visit their wives only briefly and secretly during the night.

The social difference between persons associating in a men's house is clearly expressed in the course of these activities, though occasions calling for a complete linear ranking are avoided. The chief and his lineage mates, the Pakhtuns, usually sit in an inner circle, sometimes on European type chairs, while others sit on beds or squat on the ground around them. When eating, the Pakhtuns have their meal first, leaving what remains to low status hangers-on. When thirsty, the Pakhtuns call for a glass of water, to be supplied by any low status person present. Terms of address express relative status. Etiquette further prescribes a multitude of ways in which inequality of status may be expressed.

These expressions of status difference all relate either to a single pair, or to a gross division of those present into two or three groups. More elaborate expressions of precedence are avoided. When tea is served, *two*

---

[1] Water-pots are used as percussion instruments; half filled with water, the top covered over by the left hand, they are beaten with a stick.

teapots are often used, and several cups filled and handed out at the same time. Similarly, people prefer to sit in a circle or series of concentric circles, without any rank order of seats in any one.

Some of the strategic implications of the men's house—such as the value for a chief of always having a group of men available in a fortified building—are self-evident; others will be discussed later. As a recreational centre its significance lies in the frequency and intimacy of contact which it allows between persons even at opposite extremes of the rank hierarchy. There is free give and take between the lowest and the highest. The manner in which hierarchy is expressed creates no barrier to communication. In Pathan villages with men's houses there can be no development of an elite separated from the masses; the potential members of such an elite are each engaged separately in his own men's house in intensive social intercourse with their followers and supporters. The emphasis, as throughout in Pathan social organization, is on relations between unequals, not on lateral relations with peers and equals. Thus the recreational aspect of the men's house organization defines a group recognizing the leadership of a chief, recruited locally from all castes, and maintaining a high level of internal social activity and communication between its members.

The relationship between a villager and a Pakhtun leader, whereby the former gains regular access to a men's house and becomes a member of the clique-like group that habitually congregates there, thus has the nature of an informal contract. In return for the numerous pleasures and benefits of membership, the villager must submit to the presiding chief's authority and thus forfeit an unspecified part of his political freedom. For this reason it is impossible for a person to be for any length of time simultaneously a member of several men's house groups. Situations frequently arise where a choice must be made. On the other hand, there is no necessity for a person to be a member of any men's house at all, and many villagers prefer to remain uncommitted.

SAINTS AND THEIR FOLLOWERS

Some villagers stay away from the men's house group because they prefer to place exclusive trust in a Saint by joining the group which forms around him. It has been remarked that men's house leadership is a prerogative of Pakhtuns, and is regarded as incompatible with the status of Sainthood. Nevertheless, groups which are structurally equivalent to the men's house groups do form around prominent Saints. The following of a Saint is recruited by a series of contract-like relations of religious tutelage with individual devotees. By creating a centre for instruction and conversation in his house or in the local mosque, the Saint welds these separate devotees into a co-ordinated group. In the following I shall describe these bonds of religious tutelage, particularly in relation to political activity. I should, however, emphasize that there is no clear dichotomy in terms of membership between these followings of Saints and the men's house groups. While it is practically impossible to be simultaneously a member of two men's houses, there is nothing to prevent a member of a men's house from being the disciple of a Saint. But according to their personal inclinations, most men prefer one kind of group to the other.

As a background for this description, it is necessary to discuss in some detail the Pathan conception of holy status, since it is in terms of this conception that disciples choose a Saint to follow.

There are a number of categories of descent groups claiming holy status. Of highest rank among them are *Sayyids*, the descendants of the Prophet Mohammed. The largest group is constituted by *mians*, a term applied loosely by lay Pathans to any descendant of a holy man, though strictly speaking pertaining only to the descendants of Saints of a particular grade. Holy status may also be achieved. A man of any caste may dedicate himself to religion, in the tradition of Hindu ascetics or Persian Sufis. People pursuing such a course under the instruction of a recognized Saint, are called *shaikh* or *murid*, or, upon the attainment of some degree of success, *pir*. A *pir* has in a sense changed his caste; his descendants are classed as the descendants of a Saint. Similarly, if a *mullah* successfully assumes the role of a spiritual leader, making his religious and moral teaching relevant to the social problems of his day, he may come to be regarded as a Saint (usually labelled as *faqir* in its strict meaning of a dedicated property-less man), and his descendants will be classed as the descendants of a Saint.

Prominent persons in any of these categories are called *zbarge*, literally, a Saint. For simplicity in exposition I shall apply the term Saint to all persons occupying holy status, whether prominent or not. 'Saint' in this sense serves roughly as a translation of the Pashto word *mian*, as used by persons not theologically oriented.

A note should be added regarding the proper names of Saints, some of which are cited below. Since it is considered disrespectful to address or refer to a person clearly senior, or in authority, by his personal name, circumlocutions, political titles, or kinship terms of the second ascending generation are used. This applies particularly to Saints, who are known by various terms in different circles. In citing incidents and naming persons, I shall use standard terms of reference and occasionally aliases.

The Saints of Swat are revered and respected by most of the local population. This special position and authority derives from three main sources: the ownership of the graves of their saintly ancestors which serve as shrines, their traditional role as privileged mediator and adviser to others, and their claim to spiritual leadership due to legal knowledge and moral dedication.

The Pathans of Swat proclaim themselves to be strict Sunnis, and have recently come increasingly under the influence of fundamentalist and puritan interpretations of Wahabi type. The expressed norms on such subjects as the value of prayers to intermediaries and the building and decorating of shrines are in a state of flux. In general, the more sophisticated are critical of local traditional procedures which they regard as abuses of religion, while persons of lower social status, and particularly women, place great faith in these.

A shrine (*ziārat*) consists essentially of the grave of a person of holy repute. It may be a simple grave, though it is usually slightly larger than others, decorated with pebbles, shining fragments of glass and pottery, and often equipped with an oil-lamp which is kept burning on holy nights. More important shrines are enclosed in small houses of unequal architectural distinction.

The importance of shrines lies in the religious merit (*sawāb*) to be acquired by visiting them and honouring the man buried there. This is done by praying as one passes by, by removing one's shoes if one enters the shrine area, and by making offerings of alms by the grave. The religious merit acquired is proportional to the degree of effort expended on the visit; it is greater if one takes the direct route over rough country than if one follows the road. Certain months and days of the Moslem calendar are more propitious for such visits than others.

The relative importance of shrines is not closely correlated with the reputation for piety and distinction of the Saints buried in them. Pathans adopt an experimental attitude on this point. Importance is attached to efficacy, and a solid run of visible results establishes the shrine as one to be reckoned with. One shrine west of Biha village was discovered long after the death of the Saint. A nanny goat, grazing in the graveyard, jumped over the grave, and one of her teats brushed against the mound. It immediately became infected, swelled up, and the goat died soon after. The villagers understood that there was power in the grave, and that it deserved more respect. It is now one of the major local shrines for supplications for the fertility of stock and women. Similarly, the great shrine of Thana village contains the grave of a Saint (*ghous*—one of the ninety-nine members of the select committee for the administration of the Heavens) whose saintliness was discovered long after his death. He was an unknown stranger, and was 'discovered' by a prominent holy man when a light was seen to emanate from his grave. On the other hand, the two major shrines of the whole area, that of Pir Baba at Pacha in Buner, and that of Saidu Baba (The Akhund of Swat) in Saidu Sharif in Swat, are both graves of holy men of great prominence in their time, though the position and actions of Pir Baba (Sayyid Ali Tirmizi) are known and remembered by few of the pilgrims.

The graves of persons who were murdered (*shahīd*—martyr, regardless of the circumstances of the murder), usually on the spot where the murder took place, also sometimes serve as shrines, and are invariably treated with respect. Murdered persons are believed to be still among us, invisible to human eyes. The Koran enjoins respect for such persons.

Shrines are used by the local population of both sexes as places of supplication and prayers concerning personal matters: disease, infertility, poverty, and ill luck. In connexion with such prayers, rags are tied to poles, bushes or trees by the grave, symbolic gifts of the objects desired (clay cattle, miniature children's beds, etc.) are placed there, and horns of wild goat and sheep are piled on the grave. There seems to be no elaborate belief system to explain or validate these practices. Shrines are also used as storage places for valuable objects which are difficult to transport or guard effectively (e.g. firewood, fodder, agricultural equipment, grain). Few people dare violate a sacred spot by theft. Such action is not merely a crime, it is a sin; so objects deposited by the shrine are moderately safe.

All shrines of any importance are owned and tended by a keeper (*astanadār*) who may be an adult of either sex and should properly be a lineal descendant of the dead saint. The keeper is present at the times when pilgrims usually visit the shrine, and collects the alms and offerings which they bring. Where the income from shrines is great, and there are several collateral lines of descendants, they may tend the shrines in turn, or divide the yearly income. The division is usually made according to the principle of *tanzīl*; that is, each group of relatives takes the share of the ancestor through whom they claim it, so that four sons of one brother receive the same total as one son of another. The importance of living Saints derives partly from the fact that as keepers of shrines, descendants of the interceding good spirits, themselves potential intercessors between Man and God, they are respected, consulted and placated. There are, however, many persons of recognized holy descent who have no ancestral shrine.

All persons of Saintly status are paid respect by virtue of their holy descent and position. Everyone, even the local chief, should rise when a Saint enters the room. Some persons of this status are found in nearly all Pathan villages. Because of their inherited holiness, assumed greater knowledge of law and morality, and high rank divorced from high political office, they are the traditional mediators and advisers. This role is signified by their wearing a white turban, which makes them inviolable in feud, and permits them to cross from one warring camp to the other in pursuance of their role as mediators. This privilege does not, however, prevent them carrying arms at other times. My host in Nalkot, a Sayyid usually known as Nalkot Pacha, would illustrate this point from events in his own life, and tell of the dilemma of choice, at critical moments in his career, between arms and the white turban, and even of the quick change from one to the other in the middle of battle.

The local Saints are thus expected to make use of their privileged position to maintain peace, in return for which they are given land by the landowning Pakhtun lineage. The houses of Saints are sanctuaries in time of war. On one occasion, some fifty years ago, this rule was violated during a struggle between two factions in the village of *Thana*, and six chiefs were pursued and killed in the houses of the local Saints. A ballad describing these events has the following chorus:

Chi shpag khānān pē nə khalasēgi
When six chiefs concerning do-not-find-solution
dagha Mian la sērei chā warkəri di?
these Saints to land who has-given?

i.e., Who has given land to these Saints anyway, that they should not be able to help six chiefs?

Finally, Saints and priestly scholars occupy a position of spiritual leadership which authorizes them to initiate and direct practical action in certain circumstances. Most dramatic from the Western point of view is the holy war (*jihād*), which must be sanctioned, and is usually initiated, by a person of holy status. Equally important are the rebellions led by priests and Saints against political leaders who abuse their position intolerably.

Such then are the values and conceptions from which occupiers of holy status derive their authority. The nature of the bonds between Saints and non-Saints varies with the type of authority which is emphasized. Two typical relationships are that between adviser—mediator and his follower, or that between the leader of a holy war and the soldiers of the Faith.

The famous Akhund of Swat (died 1877), though once involved in a holy war, in the Ambeyla Campaign in 1863, in the remainder of his career used the bond between adviser and follower (*murid*). Almost all the political leaders who were successful in his generation were his followers. His advice was at times of the most practical kind, and his great sanctity guaranteed his followers success. With his help a minor chief of the Babuzai, Malak Baba, rose to great heights, and with his sons dominated a major section of the Swat valley.

The traditional account tells how early in his career Malak Baba, badly outnumbered by the enemy Jula Khel, was besieged in a village above Odigram, where his section resided at the time. Malak Baba managed to escape by night, secretly crossed the mountains and came to consult the Akhund in his village of Saidu, asking him how he could avoid the shame of having all his family killed, and losing the battle. The Akhund prayed for him and then said, 'You must slaughter a cow tomorrow (it being the day of the break of the Ramadan Fast), and fight on, and all will be well.' Malak Baba managed to slip back into the besieged village, and did as the Akhund had said. For six months he fought, sustained by the cow he had slaughtered. By then the opposing party ran out of food—whereupon he supplied them. After eating his food for a day or two, they started asking themselves 'why should we fight this man who gives us food?' and so they arrived at a peaceful settlement.

Through giving such excellent advice, the Akhund's reputation was enhanced, and his successful followers widely extended the area under their, and therefore his, control. By a net of such dyadic relations with prominent chiefs, the Akhund established an influence over the area which enabled him to control its politics and even try the experiment of uniting it under the rule of a nominee of his own. The Akhund's temporary success formed the charter for the claims of his grandson, who created the present State of Swat.

Similar bonds, on a smaller scale, relate prominent contemporary Saints with local chiefs, and minor persons of holy descent with the villagers among whom they are active. In the administered districts of Peshawar, these bonds have been utilized by the Pir of Manki village to build a political machine among a modern electorate.

The bond between Saint and follower is a wholly voluntary one, established on the initiative of the follower. The Saint is consulted on points of ritual or morality, or on purely practical matters; he functions simultaneously as a father-confessor and a lawyer. His kinship with other-wordly intercessors, his role as a mediator in this life, and his piety and knowledge of Shariat Law all suit him admirably for this double role. Because of his wide contacts among high and low and the insight into human character which he develops, he is in a position to give his followers shrewd and useful advice, whether they are politically ambitious or mainly concerned with protecting their own family's life and property.

A more temporary organization may be built around persons of less established sanctity, based on the Islamic dogma of the holy war and the blessings awaiting the soldier (*ghazi*) who figures in one. This line of appeal requires considerable demagogic powers and is mainly adopted by mullahs. Essentially, it depends for its success on the presence of a fundamental conflict in the area, and the ability to play on ideals of manliness and fearlessness so as to whip up confidence among the warriors of the community. The initiator then rides the crest of the wave, living well and having great authority while it lasts. When it is spent, he passes on to another area, there to start afresh.

British publications relating to the North-West Frontier Provinces describe the activities of various such 'fanatics' in stirring up trouble in the tribal areas (e.g. Barton, 1939, pp. 105-11, etc.). Indeed, the main conflict utilized by leaders of holy wars was that between Moslems and the Christian government of India. In the Swat-Bajaur-Mohmand area, the Haji of Turangzai and his son Badshah Gul, the Faqir of Alingar, Mullah Mastan or Sartor, Mullah Powindah, and the Sandakei Mullah all fall into this category, and have temporarily achieved control of very large groups. Thus Mullah Mastan was able to mobilize a force estimated at 12,000 men at Malakand and simultaneously another of 8,000 at Chakdara (Parliamentary Papers, 1901) in 1897, shortly after these two British forts had been built in the lower Swat valley. Similar leaders, such as Sayyid Akbar of Tirah, or the Faqir of Ipi in Waziristan have gained considerable renown on other parts of the frontier.

At the time of partition, a very large proportion of the military force of British India was employed in containing these 'fanatics'. Against the advice of their predecessors, the Pakistan authorities decided to withdraw most of their troops and demolish some of the forts. In spite of this relaxation of control the activities of fanatic leaders decreased and their influence greatly diminished. Clearly, the presence of an infidel government offered a ground for them to assume authority over such large groups of men, normally subject to another, regular system of authority on a tribal, lineage basis. The only one of the holy war leaders who still retains some importance is the Faqir of Ipi, who now preaches not *jihad* but nationalism, and fights among the hills of Waziristan for *Pakhtunistan*, a projected independent Pathan state, supported by Afghanistan and India.

Such a tie-up with international politics is in no way a departure for Pathan holy leaders. They have long been surprisingly sophisticated at seeing their particular struggles and role in an international setting. As a measure of their strategic sophistication, if not of the reliability of their sources of information, the following letter is of interest. It was found by British forces in the house of a holy leader, Sayad Akbar, in Afridi tribal territory, dated 25 October 1897, and is from a fellow saint:

'Aden, a seaport which was in possession of the British, has been taken from them by the Sultan. The Suez Canal through which British forces could easily reach India in twenty days has also been taken possession of by the Sultan, and has now been granted on lease to Russia. The British forces now require six months to reach India.' (Parliamentary Papers, 1901).

Deep-seated conflicts other than that between Moslem and Christian may thus set the scene for holy men to emerge as political leaders. The great 'spiritual' leader among the Orakzai of the Kurram valley, Mahmud Akhundzada, throughout his career maintained neutrality towards the British. The Kurram area is unique in that it contains both Sunni and Shiah groups; and this is the opposition which has supplied the Akhundzada, a strict Sunni, with the necessary platform for his activities. Even the Haji of Turangzai, affectionately known in the reminiscences of British administrators as 'the stormy petrel of the Frontier', established his position through a much less spectacular conflict than that between Moslem and Infidel: he gained ascendancy over the broken lineages of Safi and Kandahari—probably pre-Pathan in origin (Wylly, 1912)— by co-ordinating them in defence against their Tarkarni overlord, the Khan of Khar (see Barton, 1939, p. 108). Miangul Gulshahzada Abdul Wadood, the grandson of the Akhund of Swat, when he formed the Swat State did much the same thing on a larger scale. The Nawab of Dir was pressing his conquests into the Swat valley, and Miangul used this crisis to justify his claim to authority and the necessity for firm leadership. Indeed the situation was such as to invite a leader of his type and he had two rivals, Jaffar Shah and the Sandakei Mullah. Characteristically, his first action on gaining control of Swat was to expel from his territory not only those who had actually opposed him, but all potential rivals of holy status.

Mention should be made of a unique colony of religious devotees, the *Mujahidin*, or warriors of the Faith, usually referred to in English as the Hindustani Fanatics (Barton pp. 39ff). This group consists of followers of the Wahabi-inspired Sayyid Ahmad of Bareilly; they established themselves as a colony in the area between the Swat and Indus rivers about 130 years ago. Non-Pathan in origin, and financially supported from the lowlands, their internal discipline and claims to high religious merit have gained them an influence disproportionate to their numbers. The colony was formed as a militant Moslem movement against Sikh oppression, but has for most of its existence been directed against British rule in India. It has at times played an important role in the history of Swat, supporting holy leaders who claimed secular powers over the area, such as the above-mentioned Jaffar Shah, and precipitating conflicts involving British punitive expeditions into the area. It was originally located at Sitana, but after one such expedition it moved further north in the Indus basin to Samasta. Its present leader is Shahzada Barktullah. Since the establish-ment of Swat State its influence in the valley has waned steadily.

Let me attempt to draw together the threads of this chapter. I have described a series of groups relevant to specific fields of activity, mainly production, recreation, and religious studies, mostly with overlapping membership and none of them explicitly political in their functions. But they differ from the kinds of grouping described in Chapters 3 and 4 in that each is characterized by an internal authority system; they are formed by a series of dyadic contracts between a pivotal person and individual subordinates. They thus define positions of leadership and vest certain persons with authority which they may use for political purposes. The following chapters will explore the way in which leaders manipulate these positions to build a political following. But first it is necessary to complete the setting by describing the general organization of local communities.

6

Land Tenure and Political Relations within Local Communities

THE MAJOR PRINCIPLES of organization have now been described. They derive variously from kinship (caste, marriage, descent groups), economic life (economic contracts, house tenancy), recreation (men's houses), ritual (life crisis associations), and religion (the followings of Saints); but they combine in a single complex network of social relations covering the Swat valley, and connecting it with the outside world. In the preceding sections, each has been described, as far as possible, separately; and to show their relevance in social life their interconnexions within a local framework must be explained. Relations to land hold the key to such understanding, for the local community is maintained by the joint dependence of all its members on land for their subsistence. An analysis of the organization of local communities must thus be prefaced by a discussion of the land tenure system.

As has been made clear above, land in Swat is concentrated in a few hands. The greater proportion is and has always been held by *Pakhtuns*, and sovereignty over large areas is claimed by descent segments of these Pakhtuns. When asked how much land he owns, a Pakhtun landowner will name a specific number of *brakhas* (literally shares); or he gives the value of the *brakha* in rupees and pice, a terminology borrowed from the Moghul tax rating system. His answer might thus be *yaunim brákha* (one and a half shares), or *dwā-Rupəi shpag paisē* (two rupees six pice). The number of pice in a rupee is 24, 32 or 64 according to the area. The area equivalent of *brakhas* and rupees varies greatly in different regions, but within any one region it is more or less uniform.

However, the area of a 'share' can never be exactly expressed in square feet. Each share or part share contains a proportion of all the different kinds of land—unirrigated, artificially irrigated and naturally irrigated (swamp) fields, walled irrigated garden, and house-sites in the village(s) (see p. 6). And since the quality of fields in each of these categories varies, adjustments are made in terms of an evaluation of the land as *trikh* (bitter) or *khōg* (sweet). Accordingly one 'share' may contain a larger area of land of inferior quality, while another 'share' will be smaller but more fertile. Ideally all land units should thus be equivalent in value, and represent a balanced selection of the different kinds of land available. A man who owns two *brakhas* thus has, approximately, twice as large a total crop as one who owns one.

Every unit of land is thought of as a 'share', a portion of a larger estate held by a descent group of Pakhtuns. This estate is referred to as *daftar*; an individual's *daftar* is his inherited share of it as a member of the descent group. There is thus a direct connexion between the descent organization and rights to land.

Traditionally, this connexion was even closer than it is now. Until the then newly-established ruler of Swat enforced permanent settlement about thirty years ago, the actual fields were periodically re-allotted in a rotational system instituted by Shaikh Malli (see p. 9). Each landowner owned, not certain fields, but the right to a certain proportion of the total area. The simplest analogue of this system is that of shares in an industrial enterprise; a shareholder does not own any specific part of the factory. Similarly, the joint estate of a descent unit of Pakhtuns is divided into an absolute number of equal shares—80, 112, 120 *brakhas*—distributed between the members. Each individual was allotted fields of various types corresponding to the number of his shares, but he did not hold these permanently. No allotment is perfectly just; with the aim of assuring perfect equivalence of shares, allotments were made for a fixed period—four, five or ten years in different regions. At the end of this time all fields were re-allotted, so that, in the course of a long cycle, all members of the group exercised rights over all fields for the same length of time.[1]

This system is generally known among Pathans as the *wesh* (division or allotment) system. It operated within each of the eleven regions shown on Map 1 on page 14 (though by 1925 the land of the Babuzai had been permanently subdivided into three areas). Each of these regions was the *daftar* of a descent segment of Pakhtuns (except the territory of the Sebujni confederacy, who nevertheless followed the same system); these descent segments are interrelated in the manner shown on Map 1 and refer to conquest history to validate their rights.

Re-allocation took place within the limits of a descent segment. Thus there were in the Nikbi khel region (see Figure 3, p. 28) approximately a thousand shareholders. The land was divided into two roughly equivalent areas, corresponding to the two primary segments of the Nikbi khel. One section included most of the tributary valley, the other stretched along the bank of the Swat river. The two segments alternated in their occupation of these areas, each spending ten years in the side valley, and then moving some ten to fifteen miles to the river's bank. Each of these sections was subdivided into three subsections corresponding to the three secondary segments of each primary descent segment. These units of land were allocated by the casting of lots. Within each subsection villages or groups

---

[1] This system is closely analogous to the musha'a system of the Near East (Patai, 1949), and has been described among Pathans by Baden-Powell (1896), who discusses the system in some detail.

of villages were allotted to tertiary segments, and within these local areas individuals received specific fields as their property for the duration of the allotment period.

A certain amount of land was withdrawn from the re-allotment cycle, to be set aside for special purposes. Such land was, and is, called *siri*, and is of four principle kinds: land permanently dedicated to the support of mosques; land given to Saints and mediators, which is withdrawn from the tribal estate and becomes the permanent private property of the Saint and his descendants; land temporarily allotted in return for services by non-landowners such as the village carpenter or blacksmith; and land temporarily granted a chief in return for his services to the community.

Such grants reduce the landed estate of the descent group, but do not change the number of traditional shares held by members. Thus every time a gift is made, the value of each share in the estate is reduced, the loss being distributed equally.

The present system of land tenure is best understood against this background. What happened in Swat State was simply that an external agent in the form of the newly established ruler declared the last temporary settlement to be permanent; the cyclical system of allotment was simply frozen at a certain moment in time, in most regions some time in the period 1920-30. All the categories of land, and the pattern of distribution of fields, remain as they were; and the permanent settlement is still so recent that most people conceive of the situation as an unusually long interval between re-allotments rather than a fundamental change.

The district of Thana lies outside Swat State, but has nevertheless followed suit to some extent. More than half the land has been permanently allotted; this is connected with the growing interest in fruit, particularly orange orchards, the cultivation of which is incompatible with the old tenure system. Most of the unirrigated land is, however, still re-allotted at four-year intervals. Throughout Swat the riceland along the river bank, which is liable to undercutting and other flood hazards, is held on temporary tenure.

This system has important implications for the meaning of ownership. Swat Pathans have a developed notion of private ownership. A man who owns land has sovereignty over it, he is the ruler of those who live on it, he can lease it on any terms to whomever he may choose, he may leave it fallow, sell it or give it away. No other person or group has rights over it, apart from the right to tax the crop, which was instituted by the ruler of the state and is not in force in the Malakand Agency. But in the traditional re-allotment system, these absolute rights were held over specific fields only for a limited period; the permanent asset was the abstract 'share'. Holding a share implies a right to participate in the assembly of the descent group and to move from area to area with it; only descent group members may hold shares. Thus, while re-allotment was still practised, landowners could freely alienate rights to fields, but only for the duration of the allotment period, when their rights lapsed; 'shares' could also be transferred, but only within the descent segment which moved as a group. Today this restriction functions differently. A Pakhtun may still not sell a 'share' to a man outside the descent group; but he may sell the land, and such sales are in fact permanent alienations. The seller cannot claim another piece of land; he has lost his inherited 'share'. But the buyer has gained only the land, not the right to participate in the assembly. In Pathan terminology the land has been converted from *daftar* (inherited estate) to *siri* (the private property of a non-Pakhtun). At present there is a steady, though still not very high, rate of such transfers, which is undermining the descent unity of the landowners. But the main framework still persists, and certainly will for at least another generation or two. If a man loses all his *daftar*, whether by transfer to fellow descent group members or by conversion to *siri*, he also loses the opportunity of exercising his rights as descent group member, and has no land rights to transfer to his descendants; in consequence the line of his descendants lose their membership in the Pakhtun group.

The periodic re-allotment of land presupposes some administrative machinery. Some formal framework, and some set of rules, are required. This formal framework takes the form, in Swat, of a hierarchy of assemblies corresponding to the land holding units. Such an assembly, both in the sense of the meeting itself, and of the group of men who meet, is known as a *jirga*. In a wider sense this word signifies any deliberative meeting. In a more particular sense it refers to meetings of the shareholders in any recognized re-allotment unit, i.e. all heads of households of a Pakhtun descent segment.

In every community of whatever size there is, therefore, a public assembly of all the Pakhtun landowners. Only the men who hold *daftar* may speak in this assembly; they are the only full citizens of the community and act as the political patrons of their followers and those who reside on their land. As will be shown in Chapter 9, politically corporate groups co-ordinate the actions of their members in their efforts to control these assemblies. But the assemblies themselves never emerge as units in corporate action; the purpose of debates is to explore the possibilities of agreement and arrive at compromises. The implementation of any agreement reached remains the responsibility of individuals, or larger corporate groups, in self-help. As a political institution, the public assembly has more in common with the tents of Panmunjom than with a Western parliament. The institution of the *jirga* can thus best be described as a set of rules governing the conduct of assemblies. Its role as a political institution can only be explained after the constitution of politically corporate groups has been analysed.

To summarize, each of the main regions of the Swat valley is controlled by a descent segment of Yusufzai Pakhtuns. The territorial segmentation of these regions corresponds to levels of segmentation in the descent system of the Pakhtuns, and to a hierarchy of public assemblies among them. But no particular sub-segment of landowners is associated with any particular local area. The Pakhtuns used to alternate in their occupation of each area, sharing the spoils of conquest and exploiting each in turn. Though for the last thirty years they have been permanently settled, the association between Pakhtuns and the larger population is in no way firm, and retains the old flavour of insecurity, military occupation and temporary exploitation. It is against this background that the role of the many other elements of organization must be understood.

Different Pakhtuns in a local area are competing partners in a privileged position; together they control a resource in the form of a limited area, the gross productivity of which, as a result of the highly developed irrigation system, is practically a constant. A Pakhtun's profits may theoretically be increased in either of two ways. All the Pakhtuns of an area may combine to exploit the non-landowners by demanding the maximum share of gross income for themselves; or an individual may extend his control over a larger proportion of the land, thus increasing his own profits at the expense of other landowners. The second of these courses is that generally adopted, as is apparent from the kinds of bonds between persons described above.

By adopting this strategy a landowner can build up common interests with a body of followers vis-à-vis rival landlords. Bonds with fellow landowners, on the other hand, are largely undeveloped. Marriages are made mostly with close relatives or outside the village altogether; membership of life crisis associations and men's houses link persons of different castes; occupational contracts and house tenancies create relationships with nonlandowners. Only the bond of common descent, implying joint rights over land in the old tenure system, links landowners of a locality.

Clearly, therefore, a permanent allotment of land must lead to the eventual breakdown of the widely ramifying descent system. This, indeed, may have been the main purpose of the ruler of Swat when he enforced settlement. The argument is strengthened by the breakdown of descent organizations in the Panjkora and Bajaur valleys which are similar to Swat in economy but do not have the land re-allotment system. Here innumerable petty feudal principalities have succeeded one another through the nineteenth and twentieth centuries.

The strategy of severe exploitation by a combination of landowners is in fact not practicable. The non-landowners are already living barely above subsistence level, and would be below it were not a part of the taxes they pay returned to them in the form of the chief's hospitality in the men's houses. Furthermore, landowners are greatly outnumbered by nonlandowners, and could not maintain themselves as a group if the latter were united against them. It is by becoming the leader of the non-landowners, not by turning them against himself, that a Pakhtun landowner maintains his position.

To the sedentary villagers, whether tenants, craftsmen, or others, the

Pakhtun represents an unnecessary imposition. They have their own web of kinship ties, their local associations for life crises; between them they have all the skills and man-power necessary to maintain the economic system; they have built and must keep up their own houses, they know the fields and the irrigation system better than the Pakhtuns.

The problem that faces the Pakhtun—most dramatically in the traditional re-allotment system, on suddenly finding himself face to face with a couple of thousand unknown persons, his potential allies or enemies for the next ten years—is how to make himself indispensable to the villagers, how to tie as many of them as possible to himself. The answer is found in the Pakhtun's claim to ownership of all land, and in an organization based on this assumption, using the different kinds of contracts described in the previous chapters. The non-landowners have not any such political organization as would enable them to unite and seize the land. They are merely a kind of sea of politically unorganized peasants and craftsmen. In the following chapters, I shall analyse the way in which the landowners build up their hierarchy of command and organize individuals into corporate groups for purposes of defence. But this analysis may be clearer if I anticipate its conclusions and sketch the relation between local communities and the political organization. The actions of prominent leaders serve to create foci of authority within communities, rather than clearly delimited units embracing sections or the whole of such communities. To pursue the metaphor, the landowner faced with the sea of politically undifferentiated villagers proceeds to organize a central island of authority, and from this island he attempts to exercise authority over the surrounding sea. Other landowners establish similar 'islands', some with overlapping spheres of influence, others having unadministered gaps between them. In other words, the leaders among the landowners do not formally organize the whole community into a single, systematic political structure. This relates to the fact, often repeated in the previous chapters, that most relations between landowners and villagers have the form of voluntary contracts.

Within such a framework of ideas, let us adopt, for the moment, the point of view of non-landowners. Each separate villager clearly sees himself as exercising a choice. Either he may make every possible contract with one leader and so to speak, join his 'island'. Or he may establish no contract with any leader, and thus remain entirely outside the different fields of authority. Both alternatives have readily apparent advantages and disadvantages. In the former the villager makes himself subject to the whims of a leader, but profits materially and obtains protection. In the latter, he remains free of external control at the price of considerable material discomfort, and must also manage without any protection against aggression.

In fact most villagers compromise by making some only of the possible contracts with the landowner, and thus come within the sphere of influence of a leader without being completely identified with him. The decision which contracts to make depends on many factors, among them personal inclinations, and the offers made him by landowners; and any attempt to analyse the bases of such decisions would thus meet with great difficulties. It should however be remembered that a great number of villagers are very poor. The rights which are obtained through these various contracts—to work in a field, to live in a house, to call for assistance against persons who threaten his family and property—are thus of great value to them. In return they have only their services to offer.

Through such a system of organization any landowner can put himself at the head of a group of dependants. But since landowners are also divided, each leader needs supporters against his rivals. The efforts of leaders to build up political followings thus reflect the tensions between groups as much as the requirements of group discipline. The present study approaches the political system through the analysis of the actions whereby leaders are able to assume and maintain their position.

7

Authority and Following of Chiefs

GENERAL DISCUSSION OF LEADERSHIP

PATHANS, when discussing political events or contemplating political action, are naturally aware of the existence of definite alignments of people who can be mobilized as corporate units in the event of conflicts. But Pathans were as unable as myself to see any simple principle for the recruitment of such groups. One does not hear reference to 'my descent group', 'my association', 'my caste' or even 'my men's house' in such contexts—the reference is always to 'the party of so and so'. The activities of groups are discussed in terms of the actions of their leaders. From Pathan descriptions of conflicts, one might think they were duels. One description, taken down verbatim through an interpreter, reads as follows:

'There were four Khans: Mohammed Awzəl Khan, Taj Mohammed Khan, Amir Khan and Biha Malak. They invited the Nawab of Dir to invade upper Swat. He came and supported them, and they ruled the Sebujni and Shamizai. The other party was the Darməi Khan. He and the Badshah (later the founder of Swat State) were getting ready. When they invaded, Khan Bahadur Sahib, who was the brother's son of Taj Mohammed Khan, rebelled against his uncle and joined the Bahshah—but this he only did after the Nawab had been driven out, and Taj Mohammed Khan had been weakened; he slowly took over one village after another, ate his way through the whole thing. The four old Khans fled to Dir, but some later returned. Their rifles were confiscated, their movable property taken, but their inherited land was returned to them, except that which was claimed by their relatives.'

As a matter of fact, these conflicts involved armies of the order of ten thousand soldiers, and scores of very prominent chiefs. None of the four old Khans ever returned to Swat, but hundreds of their followers did (though most of their followers did not accompany them on their flight in the first place), and the number of rifles confiscated ran into thousands.

When speaking of corporate groups, I shall be referring to groups capable of concerted action under the direction of a leader or a number of co-ordinating leaders. According to Maine's definition (Maine, 1861), corporate groups should persist in perpetuity, independently of the life and death of individuals. This is true of the groups in question, though not unequivocally so: a great turnover of personnel is possible through death or secession, but the death of the leader creates a crisis, since conflicts over succession to leadership frequently dissolve the group.

The criterion of common jural responsibility, applied by Fortes (1953, pp. 25-6) in his discussion of lineages as corporate groups, is also only roughly applicable. Since policy is determined predominantly by the leading members, responsibility too is allotted on a graded scale. Followers who are mere tools in a leader's hand have but little responsibility, even for their own actions. It is the part in the decision, not in the action, which confers responsibility; thus the members of groups share jural responsibility only in proportion to their authority.

There are fundamentally two kinds of political leaders among Pathans, which I have called respectively chiefs and Saints.

Chiefs may hold several different titles, but by far the most common is *Khān*. This title may be used as a term of address and respect to any landowner, and is occasionally also given as a personal name. When necessary, a chief in the political sense is distinguished from such chiefs-by-courtesy by the phrase *da tāṛne Khān*—'chief of the fortress'. Alternatively, a chief may be known as *málak*. This title refers properly to a lineage headman, and is used extensively in other Pathan areas. In Swat it is going out of use, as has the office of lineage headmanship itself, though it is occasionally retained as a title. A *málak* should in general rank lower than a *khān*, but as a result of the wide use of khan as a courtesy title, this difference is not always clear, and the ranks may even be reversed. Finally, a chief of very great prominence and authority over a large area, or state, is known as *Nawāb*, as the Nawab of Dir, various lesser Nawabs of Bajaur, and the Nawab of the State of Amb. Common to all chiefs is their claim to some kind of lineal inheritance of the title, their membership in the Pakhtun caste, and their dominance in the region by virtue of their prominence as a *daftar*-holding landlord.

Saints also may hold one of several titles, usually *Pīr*, *Bāba*, or *Pācha*. *Sāhib* is frequently used as a title of address and reference to all persons of holy descent, but also occasionally to chiefs or other prominent persons. The name of the grade of sainthood held, such as *Sayyid*, *Akhundzada*, *Mian*, may also be used as a title by a Saint. The ranking of these various titles is not agreed upon.

Politically corporate groups are created by the actions of leaders. Any such group consists of all the persons whom a leader is able to mobilize in the event of conflict. Its limits are undefined except in relation to the leader, and its solidarity derives from the latter's authority. This authority may be attained in various ways. Persons may be committed by previous arrangements to support a given leader. Their services may be bought by gifts and promises. Their support may be won by the leader's prestige and moral or ethical fitness. Or, finally, their support may be compelled by force.

Previous commitments of followers are mainly those arising from house tenancy or occupational contracts. In these relationships the leader is in a position to exercise control by threatening to withdraw benefits, and the follower, on the other hand, can expect to obtain advantages through his leader's success. The ability to give gifts depends on superior wealth, and so ultimately on the control of land. Diréct force is of limited use in winning supporters, since it presupposes a strong following. Terrorism designed to cause secessions from the ranks of opponents is sometimes effective.

In most parts of Swat there is no necessary connexion between the different relationships that imply political submission. There is thus nothing to prevent the more peripheral members of one leader's following from having some commitments to another leader, particularly if the two are allies, or belong to the different categories of chief and Saint. Furthermore, there is nowhere any *a priori* reason why a man should attach himself to any particular leader. The position of a leader is thus never secure; his following may swell or shrink almost without warning. Since leaders are permanently in competition, the sources of their authority are most clearly exhibited in situations of conflict.

The objects of strife among Pathans are, according to a Pakhto proverb, *zin, zer, zamīn*—'women, gold, land'. *Zamīn*, land, is the ultimate source of livelihood for leader and follower alike; its acquisition and retention are in the interest of both. His ownership of land gives the leader power over those who depend on it. *Zer*, gold, stands for riches in general, which, utilized in making gifts or bribes, gives authority over others. Finally, *zin*, women, are a source of conflicts in so far as family honour is involved in the conduct of sisters and wives. Such conflicts are regarded as the ultimate tests of a man's honour, martial valour and ability to command.

In what follows I choose to look at these conflicts, not as disputes to be settled by recourse to law, but as political contests. This emphasis corresponds to the point of view generally adopted by my informants. It is also particularly suitable in the empirical situation, since the outcome of such conflicts is decisive for the political careers of leaders.

Followers seek those leaders who offer them the greatest advantages and the most security. With this aim they align themselves behind a rising leader who is successfully expanding his property and field of influence. In contrast, the followers of leaders who are on the defensive suffer constant annoyance from the members of the expanding groups. Under this pressure they tend to abandon their old leaders and seek protection and security elsewhere. Leaders are thus forced to engage in a competitive struggle. A position of authority can be maintained only through a constant successful struggle for the control of sources of authority.

THE CHIEF'S SOURCES OF AUTHORITY

The title of *Khān*, chief, even apart from its extended courtesy use, does not denote incumbency óf any formal office. There is no recognised hierarchy of positions to be filled by successful pretenders. The title merely implies a claim to authority over others; it is a statement of a person's willingness to lead. Chiefs compete with each other for followers. The main sources of influence over followers are control of the sources of livelihood, the distribution of wealth, martial valour in defence of the family honour, and also in some areas, an organizational device known as the *təlgeri* system.

Land forms the basis for the whole system of organization in Swat. Quite apart from the profits it supplies in the form of rent, its owner, by his mere possession, gains authority and control over numerous persons. The whole population of Swat is directly dependent on land in some form or other; and non-landowners can only gain access to it through agreements with landowners. The two important categories of land in the present context are dwellings and agricultural land. A dwelling in this sense is known as a *kōṭa*, and consists of a house-site in the village area, and at least the four walls of the house structure. The roof-beams are private movable property, and are often removed if the dwelling changes hands. Every family must have a dwelling of this kind, and persons who do not own land obtain one through a house tenancy contract (pp. 50ff). Such a contract places the tenant in a relation of dependence on the owner; it also gives the owner a certain political authority over the tenant, who becomes his client for administrative purposes. But the tie of clientage is not exclusive; the house tenant may seek other political patrons for protection against the house-owner. Nevertheless, the house-owner is in a clear position of political dominance over the tenant. The possession of agricultural land is a political asset in the same way. Though no political clientage is implied in land tenancy contracts (p. 44), the tenant depends on the land for his livelihood, and the power of eviction gives the landowner a hold on him.

The ownership of land is thus a direct source of political influence. An increase in land holdings implies an increase in such influence; indeed the possession of extensive lands is a basic requirement for any kind of security in a position of ascendancy. The competition between chiefs is thus largely for the control of land, and the acquisition of land is an important move in a political ascent. Land may be obtained in four ways: by inheritance, as a reward for political service, by purchase, or by violence or threats. These four methods merit some attention.

Real property passes in inheritance from a man to his closest agnatic relatives in the order: son, father, son's son, father's father, brother, father's brother, brother's son, father's brother's son. The presence of a person in any one category excludes the succeeding categories, so where there are one father's brother and four brother's sons, the father's brother takes the whole estate. Thus it is only groups of brothers who ever share an estate. In the division among them, each receives an equal share; there is no preference for the first- or last-born son.

Sometimes a descent group segment of Pakhtun landowners may recognize a single leader. In such cases, the chief may be vested with a certain area of land in return for his services as leader; such land is called *pargái siri*. During his lifetime, it forms part of his private property. On his death, however, it is not divided between his heirs, but passes as a unit to his successor in the position of leader. Such *pargái* estates form the nuclei in the formation of *khānates*, petty principalities, by preventing the fragmentation of property between multiple heirs. They are not, however, a regular feature of the tenure system in the Swat valley.

Land is a scarce resource in Swat and there are always eager prospective buyers; consequently the price, in cases of outright sale, is extremely high. But people hesitate to sell real property, since this is tantamount to renouncing all claim to high status. Nevertheless, chiefs occasionally find themselves in such great need of funds that they sell part of their land, hoping to be able to regain it later. The volume of such transfers is difficult to estimate, as both parties generally maintain a discreet silence.

Finally, land may be obtained by force or deception. There are various recognized methods.

Where there has been permanent settlement, a stronger landlord generally attempts to encroach on the land of his weaker neighbours by the slow but steady technique of ploughing the borderpath between the fields. These borders are marked by a low wall. In the irrigated rice-lands this is less than a foot wide, and serves as a retaining wall for irrigation water and a raised path for reaching the further paddy fields. In the natural-flow irrigation system, fields are usually very small, and the 'share' system makes for extreme fragmentation and dispersal of holdings. The total length along which one man's fields adjoin those of others is considerable, and the amount that can be gained by twice yearly adding one furrow along this whole length may be spectacular in the course of a generation. The strategic advantage of this technique is that there is no critical moment in its execution when dramatic counteraction is precipitated. Pathan landowners exercise constant vigilance against it.

As there is no survey or registration of land holdings among Swat Pathans, all claims to land must be supported by witnesses and boundaries are delimited by the decision of mediators or assemblies. In the course of recent history considerable landed estates have been gained and lost, and there is a confusion of conflicting claims to many fields, which refer for their validation to different periods of time. This offers a fertile field for controversy, of which chiefs may take advantage by backing the claims of small landowners. The chief contracts to carry another man's case successfully through the assembly or to a mediator, and to protect the claimant against foul play by his more powerful opponents. In return for this service, the chief asks for a half share of the property concerned, to be discreetly passed on to him at a later date. The small claimant has nothing to lose and half a field to gain by this arrangement; he can moreover expect his relationship with the powerful chief to bear additional fruits in the future. An influential chief can thus use his influence directly to enlarge his own estate, as well as that of his followers. This technique is extensively used today.

Finally, powerful chiefs can frighten or force people to sell or abandon their claim to land. This method was apparently popular in the past, though under present conditions it is no longer prevalent. However, I was able to collect numerous examples. Almost inevitably, it leads to feud, since many small landowners are prepared to be killed in defence of their land rather than give it up. The simplest procedure was outright murder followed by occupation of the murdered man's estate. Less blatant is 'sale' under duress, or the quiet abandonment of rights. This technique requires secrecy, lest public opinion should rally in support of the weaker party. In the traditional re-allotment system it was difficult to maintain such secrecy. According to informants, one famous Khan, who amassed a great deal of land by this means, found a gentlemanly solution to this problem: he gave the other chiefs of his village first choice at each re-allotment, retaining what remained after they had all received their shares, so that his own share was never counted up.

Rights to land are thus the subject of considerable dispute. A conflict of this kind is known as *shar*. If, in such a situation, the weaker party refuses to give in, he can adopt either of two courses, both very dangerous to him; feud, which may lead to his own death, or the mobilization of support among other leaders, which may lead to total defeat. His decision and that of the leaders whose support he seeks, are political decisions and can only be explored in the wider political setting described in Chapter 9. Apart from these controls, there is an upper limit to every chief's aggressiveness, since he must always keep the number of his enemies lower than the total force of his following.

Within these limits, chiefs are constantly engaged in attempts to increase their landed property. Conflicts over land have the advantage, from the chief's point of view, that they automatically involve the self-interest of many of his non-Pakhtun followers. If his title is threatened, their rights are threatened too; if his property is expanded, their potential profits are expanded as well. Conflicts over land mobilize all the tenants of the land-owners concerned in groups based on common interest; they divide co-villagers and identify followers more closely with their leaders. They enable the landowner to cement the unity of his own following by leading them in activities where their common interest is clear.

Rights to land are thus an important direct source of political authority, but they are not the only such source. Land is also the basis of wealth, and Pathans see wealth as a second source of conflicts and thus, in this analysis, of authority.

The people of Swat, though till recently, and to a considerable extent still, living in a non-monetary economy, have long been familiar with coinage, and had access to a certain volume of exchange media. In the valley bottom, the farmer ploughing his fields often turns up Bactrian coins, and children and adults alike dream of finding vast hidden hoards. At least since the beginning of Moghul times, doles and bribes have been paid the tribesmen by the successive governments of the plains, and some external trade has augmented these sources. Gold-dust and coins have thus long been familiar as a measure of value and medium of exchange; however, in the proverb referred to earlier, 'gold' is taken to refer to any conveniently movable form of wealth.

The authority of a chief depends very directly on the manipulation of such wealth, and chiefs use their yearly income to support their position and assure themselves a following in several ways, by bribes, payments, gifts and hospitality. The cultural significance of these different kinds of transaction must be understood if their political role is to be understood.

Payment in return for services implies a relationship of inequality (see p. 48) between the partners to the transaction, and responsibility on the part of him who pays for the actions of him who performs the service.

Gifts can be cancelled out by an equivalent return, and do not imply any authority of the giver over the receiver. Gift giving is used to express relationships of friendliness and rough equality—never to shame the recipient. Unilateral gift-giving expresses a difference in status between the giver and the receiver, but does not effectively put the recipient under an obligation to respond to the command of the giver, as does the payment of bribes or salaries.

Hospitality is, in a sense, a special variety of gift-giving, with the added factor of commensality. Commensality implies solidarity, and the recipient of food is under an obligation to respect his host, and to support him in times of need. To abandon persons with whom one has shared a meal in case of trouble is dishonourable, to stick by them is meritorious. But no sanctions can be brought to bear on dishonourable persons, and the loyalty and solidarity that are expressed in commensality need not be very deep-seated.

It might seem from this that gifts and hospitality would be less important than bribes and payments in supporting claims to authority. As a matter of fact, the reverse is true. Bribes and payments create relationships which render them onerous or hazardous. Gifts and hospitality, on the other hand, are of prime importance in the building up of a political following. The reason for this is to be found in a consideration of the order of magnitude involved.

To show this we need to examine the sources and amount of a chief's income. The sources are diverse, and include income from the political position itself, from the outlying land and pasture areas controlled by the chief, and from his own agricultural land.

Of sources of income deriving from the position of chiefship, the following are important. Direct subsidies have long been paid by governments in the plains: two chiefs in Thana receive 1,500 rupees per year and a third 3,000. When this payment was instituted, before 1900, the importance of such a large outside source of money income for the chief was very considerable. Since Swat was officially recognized by British India in 1926, all external subsidies have been paid directly to its ruler, just as they were and are also paid to the Nawab of Dir, who receives 50,000 rupees a year. The ruler of Swat redistributes these and other funds in subsidies to the chiefs who support him. Each of these receives an annual grant which depends on his importance and influence; the amounts range from 300 to 2,000 rupees. These fixed subsidies have largely replaced the older system of claiming head-tax and protection money from caravans passing through the chief's demesne. For example, lumber merchants formerly had to pay the chiefs controlling the banks of the Swat river for the right to float timber, at the rate of 6,000 rupees yearly to the Aka-Maruf and Barat khel chiefs of Babuzai. Fines imposed on their subjects, in the traditional system as well as in Swat State, form another source of income. In the traditional system as it exists in present-day Thana, such fines are used for public or political purposes by the chiefs in power, while in Swat State chiefs receive a cut of every fine collected from their subjects.

The outlying land and pasture areas contribute a variable, but at times very important, amount to the chief's total income. Forests and mountains are a source of revenue, since nomadic herdsmen have to pay for the right to the pastures; they pay also for grazing rights in the stubble and embankments of the rice-fields after harvest. The fee is calculated in numbers of buffalo, on the equation 20 sheep = 4 cows = 1 buffalo. It is generally paid in clarified butter, though the nomads who visit administered districts and have money income in the winter often pay in Pakistan rupees. Such fees are generally shared by all landowners in proportion to the size of each one's *daftar*; in some areas, however, they are paid into a fund which is administered by the chief.

Finally, as one of the main landlords of his village, the chief collects the landowner's share of the crops from his own fields. Even a minor chief—and there are generally several in any one village—must be a landlord of some importance to be able successfully to claim authority: of the small chiefs with whom I came into contact, none had less than five labourers working in their fields and depending on these fields for their and their families' subsistence. As the agricultural labourer takes one fifth and the landowner four fifths of the crop, this implies a gross income for even the smallest chief, from his agricultural land alone, twenty times greater than that of the average tenant. Prominent chiefs own ten times as much land, and a few even more.

The difference in the yearly income from agriculture of a tenant and a prominent chief is truly spectacular, and at harvest-time staggering amounts of grain are deposited in the storehouses of a chief. Most of this wealth remains in the form of grain, which indeed serves as a medium of

exchange and remuneration. But in parts of the Swat valley where communications have been developed an increasing quantity is sold to the
grain-markets of Peshawar. At the time of my visit, one of my acquantances
among the more prominent chiefs had an approximate income of 50,000
Pakistan rupees (then about £5,000) from the sale of grain. The average
villager's income is about 300 rupees. But this development of exports is
recent, and has not yet gone very far. Most of the agricultural produce of
Swat circulates in an internal system of exchange, and is consumed in the
area.

A prominent chief thus disposes of literally a hundred times the wealth,
both perishable and imperishable, which is required to satisfy the reasonable
needs of his own family.

Not so the majority of the village population. The Swat valley is densely
populated, and pressure on land is great. A considerable proportion of the
population lives near subsistence level. The birth rate is fairly high, but
so is the child mortality rate. Pathan parents are aware that the high
mortality among their children is due to insufficient or inappropriate food,
and to the poverty that prevents them from procuring sufficient clothes,
medicines and protective amulets. Wealthy families do not suffer these
hardships, and the sibling groups among the wealthy are larger.

This picture is based on my own impressions and the statements of
informants. In poor families one frequently sees small sibling groups
spanning an age differential of twenty years. Where I was able to obtain
the information, I found that in such cases there had been numerous conceptions and births, but a high rate of infant and child mortality. The
larger sibling groups of wealthy people are in part the result of polygamy,
but informants agreed that full sibling groups are also larger, mainly
owing to their better diet.

In the idiom of Swat Pashto, the world is divided into two kinds of
people: *mōṛ saṛi*, 'satisfied men', and *wúge saṛi*, 'hungry men'. The
'satisfied men' have enough food in their storehouses to feed the families
of scores of 'hungry men' throughout the year. The chief, by his over-
whelming wealth, is thus not only in a position to offer occasional gifts
and hospitality; he can really make a substantial contribution to the
subsistence of his followers. If offered such a contribution over a period of
time, a poor man inevitably bases his domestic economy on it. The
possibility of its being cut off becomes a major threat.

It is against this background that the importance of gifts and hospitality
as a source of the chief's political authority must be understood. Gift-
giving and hospitality are potent means of controlling others, not because
of the debts they create, but because of the recipient's dependence on their
continuation. A continuous flow of gifts creates needs and fosters dependence, and the threat of its being cut off becomes a powerful disciplinary
device. In contrast to the giving of salaries and bribes, which places
responsibility on the chief who pays, gifts and hospitality give a chief

political control over followers without saddling him with responsibility for their actions.

The scene of most gift-giving and hospitality is the men's house (see pp. 52ff). Here the efficacy of the gifts is enhanced by their public transfer; the chief's character as a lavish giver becomes known to outsiders, who are thus attracted to visit his men's house.[1]

Distributions of durable wealth are fairly rare today in the Swat men's houses, though the alms enjoined by the Koran are often given by the chief in his men's house, thereby contributing to his political, as well as his religious, merit. Gifts to individuals of some single valuable item are much more frequent. In the old days, according to informants, gift-giving in the men's house was much more lavish, and Jamroz Khan of Babuzai, for one, used to walk into his men's house with his shirt-front full of rupees, giving the money out in handfuls to all those present. Hospitality, on the other hand, is still maintained at a lavish level. Food is provided for all travellers, visitors and needy persons; feasts are given at which rice, chicken, clarified butter and soured milk are consumed from large flat trays by circles of hungry men. Around them hover the little boys, to descend on the remains and lick the trays when the men have finished. I was not able to collect any detailed figures on the economics of a chief's household and feast-giving in the men's house. But since the lack of transport facilities in most places prevents the export of grain on any scale, practically all the locally produced grain must be consumed in the village, and a large proportion of it in feasts in the men's houses.

The importance for chiefs of the bonds created by hospitality is best seen by their actions when under political pressure, or when their income falls short of its usual level. In such circumstances the hospitality offered in the men's house is intensified rather than reduced; and if a sale of real property can be negotiated without too much publicity, the amount realized will be expended so as to maintain this higher level.

This condition was exemplified by several chiefs at the time of my visit. One such chief is the senior son of a former leader of great importance. He is himself fairly prominent, but he is subject to irregular loss of land, and frequent fines by the Ruler of Swat. Through all this he maintains a higher level of hospitality than any of the other chiefs in the area; in the

[1] This view of the connexion between the institution of the men's house and the political activities of chiefs is supported by the changes that have taken place in the neighbouring Peshawar District. In that area, which formerly had an economic and social system similar to that of Swat today (Elphinstone, 1839, vol. II, pp. 27-8), the registration of titles and establishment of a police system under British administration progressively guaranteed tenure and thus eliminated the necessity for landowners to maintain political supremacy. At the same time, the introduction of an effective monetary economy made possible the conversion of perishable wealth into cash. The result of these inter-connected changes was the disappearance from Peshawar District of the men's house. With improved communications and greater security, similar changes are taking place in Swat, though at the time of fieldwork they had not yet proceeded very far.

course of the last ten years he has sold extensive lands to feed the many visitors to his men's house. I discussed this policy with him, and he was fully aware that his actions were progressively reducing his yearly income and thus aggravating the crisis. 'On the other hand,' he said, 'if people stop sitting in my men's house, I shall lose the land even faster; only this constant show of force keeps the vultures at bay.' The substantial group of goldsmiths and muleteers living as landowners in the village of Worejo is another example. This group of small landowners has come into being because the Manki khel chiefs of the village have repeatedly sold land in order to finance hospitality, and have maintained their political position by living beyond their income.

The chief's hospitality in his men's house makes his followers dependant on him as a source of food—for very many of the regular visitors could not do without the numerous free meals provided there. The chief also establishes a reputation for lavishness, shows himself capable of profitable management of his estates, and in general gains prestige as a desirable leader. Followers flock to his men's house and his political influence increases. Through this influence he can expect to enlarge his lands and gain greater wealth, ever more followers and still greater influence. At the same time, his followers are welded into a group the solidarity of which is reinforced by commensality, which puts them all under a moral obligation to support one another. Persons without common interests, or even with opposed interests, such as tenant and herdsman, or shopkeeper and labourer, in this way become members of a viable unit under external pressure.

HONOUR, AND CONFLICTS IN DEFENCE OF HONOUR

In addition to possessing lands and wealth, a chief must command respect. His relations to his various dependents are almost entirely such that they may be broken at will by either party. Thus all Pathan males, except the few slaves, are free at any time to throw their lot in with a new leader, to hitch their wagon to a rising star. A poor man may be dependent on the hospitality and gifts of a chief for his sustenance; but if a new chief promises to give more, and has more to give, this reason for remaining with the old chief disappears. Similarly, a chief may be wealthy in inherited lands; but if he is losing this land to rival chiefs, he will be short of land to offer his followers on tenancy contracts, and his hold over them will be reduced. A man choosing a leader to whom he commits himself politically will evaluate his wealth and land and hospitality; but he must also evaluate the chief's ability to cope with critical situations. Thus the intangible factor of prestige or reputation becomes a major source of authority, an important means by which a political pretender rallies supporters. The qualities are evaluated in terms of the polar opposites *izat* honour, and *sharm*—shame. The ideal personality of a leader is virile and impetuous, given to extremes rather than compromise, sometimes unwise, but always brave. All leaders do not live up to this ideal equally well; but their actions are judged in relation to it, and they gain authority and attract followers in proportion to their performance as measured by such standards.

Honour, in this sense, is thus a matter of major concern to political pretenders—as indeed to every self-respecting man—and conflicts in defence of honour become tests of a man's qualifications to leadership. As a source of conflict a threat to a man's honour is thus as important as a threat to his possession of land. Pathans express this in terms of a 'pure case'—the defence of the honour of wives and sisters; hence the proverbial reference to women as a source of conflict. Actually any insult, any action or condition which 'shames' a Pathan, requires him to defend his honour, if he is not to suffer permanent loss of respect and status.

This code of honour, in its positive aspect, is difficult to analyse. Honour as a source of authority is certainly conceptually distinct, in the eyes of a Pathan, from such other sources of authority as land ownership and wealth. It is possible, to a degree, to be honourable yet poor. More commonly a chief may be rich yet lacking in honour, and this seriously affects the extent of his political authority. Such failings are constantly discussed, in terms such as: 'He may be wealthy (*maldār*), but he's a woman (*khəze*).'

The concepts of honour and shame relate to particular actions, to the way in which a situation is dealt with, and not to the circumstances of the situation. By implication, the ideal is most clearly expressed in the idealized descriptions of past heroes. An example is a description of Jamroz Khan by one admirer: 'He was an enormous man, powerful, with a bristling moustache. He used to eat a whole ox-liver for breakfast. He would keep his eye on anyone who was gaining power; so he would say to his men: "Look here, how are you serving me, look at that man gaining influence and power!"—and the next day the news would spread in the bazaar that the man was dead.' The ideal is also clearly exemplified in the characterization of persons by Ghani Khan (1947).

In the present context we are concerned with honour and shame as measures of the relative qualifications of political pretenders. As in the case of land and wealth, those ideal qualifications of leadership which involve honour emerge most clearly in cases of conflict.

The only successful defence of honour is revenge, equal to or beyond the extent of the original insult, so as to re-establish parity or gain an advantage vis-à-vis one's rival. As in the discussion of conflicts over land, we are here concerned not with the legal but the political aspect of the conflict. The following discussion of self-help and homicide thus refers to the political relevance of such actions, interpreted by Pathans in terms of honour and shame.

Revenge in defence of honour may vary, depending on the magnitude of the insult, from seizure of the opponent's property or of hostages, beating him up, or, in serious cases, blood revenge. In other words, it requires a show of superior force by the insulted person. Revenge may therefore be taken by the man himself or by his followers acting on his behalf. The action of his friends and allies does not remove the shame as effectively as recourse to force by himself. The man who manages to extract a proper revenge when shamed has defended his honour, proved his worth and demonstrated his ability to defend his own interests. Such a man is chosen as leader by many, and is able to command the respect and obedience of these followers through their confidence in his ability to defend their interests as well as his own.

The seizure of property, for example taking cattle in compensation for a theft, is usually left to ordinary men, tenants and nomads. Such petty matters do not bring honour to chiefs. A generation ago, when raids were made on a larger scale, and relations between distant persons were not as regularized as they are today, the seizure of property, and also of hostages (*bōṭa*), was more frequent. Hostages were held to ransom until the property claimed was returned. The hostage might be a person connected in any way with the man against whom one had a claim, the assumption being that his relatives would put pressure on the principal to return the property.

The main method of defending honour is by blood revenge, *badəl*. A state of conflict involving blood revenge is known as *pokhto*—this implies the deepest form of enmity, but for long periods need not lead to action of any kind except complete social avoidance. A state of unresolved blood feud can go on for many years, but lead to no more than one or two murders in any one generation (see Appendix, case 2).

The causes of feud are various, since a revenge murder is the appropriate action in defence of honour after any serious insult. In the first place, any unavenged murder is a stain on the honour of the dead man's family. This does not apply to men killed in open battle (*jang*, see p. 122), but only to cases of deliberate murder. Secondly, fornication or adultery with a woman, if it becomes the subject of common gossip, reflects on the honour of her male relations; her kinsmen, particularly brothers and sons, and her husband, can only wipe out the stain by avenging themselves on the seducer. Further, grievous bodily harm deliberately caused in a brawl or by attack, is a serious insult and should properly be revenged by killing (Appendix, case 3); and any other action which in the situation is understood to constitute a major insult is, by the Pathan code of honour, proper justification for blood revenge (e.g. Appendix, case 2).

The legal attitude differs from this in some respects. By Islamic law, as interpreted by Swat tribal councils or religious experts, murder is justified in the case of talion revenge, and in cases of adultery, when however both adulterer and adulteress must be killed. In other cases, blood revenge is not legally justified. If such cases are brought before lineage councils in Swat, or before the Ruler of Swat State, the man who resorts to feud will be fined; but his prestige will have been enhanced and his honour defended by his action none the less.

The responsibility—or privilege—of avenging a murder devolves on the man who inherits the property of the murdered person. If for some reason the heir fails in this duty, action may be taken by any male agnate related as first paternal cousin to the dead man, or closer (Appendix, case 1). Needless to say, maternal relatives have no part in the shame, nor in the honour of a successful revenge. A mother's brother may become involved in the fighting, since his men's house is often used as a place of refuge for persons escaping blood revenge (e.g. Appendix, case 3); but this is chosen as an asylum precisely because he is not involved in the feud, and an attack on his men's house by the revengers would increase the number of their opponents.

In cases where a man has been shamed and not killed, the shame is still shared by his close agnates, and his honour defended equally by them and by himself (e.g. Appendix, case 5).

Similarly, the responsibility for the consequences of an act is shared by several persons. The doer himself, or rather he who made the decision that the action should be taken, is considered responsible. But just as shame reflects on the whole group of close agnates, giving all up to the third degree an equal right to revenge a murder, so the responsibility for an act is shared in attenuated form by the close agnates of the doer. The degree of division of responsibility varies somewhat with the nature of the act, and also appears to have undergone change during the last generation. There is a general tendency to direct the revenge for insults, as opposed to homicides, strictly against the insulter himself; so that his agnates, if careful not to provoke the aggrieved party, are subject to retaliation only if they publicly express their complicity in, or approval of, the insult. Yet in Appendix, case 3, we see a paternal uncle unable to divest himself of responsibility for bodily harm caused to another by his nephew, in spite of his public repudiation of the act.

In cases of murder, the murderer retains the major responsibility for his act; but his father, brother or son, and to less extent father's brother and paternal cousin, share in the responsibility and are acceptable substitutes in revenge, especially if the murderer is out of reach because, for example, he has fled the country.

Informants agreed that responsibility in former days was distributed more equally between the murderer and his closest agnates, and was extended somewhat further, and that the tendency in the last generation or two has been towards the restriction of responsibility to the actor himself. This is in line with the general political trend whereby descent groups are losing their corporate political functions, and also with the legal principles examplified in the courts of the neighbouring administered territories. A wide lateral extension of responsibility within whole lineage segments is, however, foreign to the Swat Pathan system.

It will be apparent from this description that the Swat Pathan pattern of blood revenge is not governed by the principle of talion; that is to say, the damage inflicted need not be equal to the damage suffered. I never heard any idea expressed of the justice of equivalence in retaliation. People are concerned rather with a man's right to defend every aspect of his social personality. Revenge in excess of talion is exemplified in Appendix, case 1, where after a successful retaliatory murder the aggrieved party continued its revenge by destroying property, after which the agnates of the murderer were still required to offer submission and sue for peace. An even more extreme example was encountered in the neighbouring Kohistan area, where two murders were committed in revenge for one—the first by a more distant agnate of the murdered man, the second by his son, who had been absent when the murder took place, but at his return, as the closest relative of the murdered man, still had the recognized 'right' to revenge (Barth, 1956, p. 45). It is the successful revenge itself, the show of superiority implied by superior force, which is sought, since this constitutes a successful defence of honour and thus repairs the damage to the personalty by re-establishing the prestige of those concerned. For the same reason, monetary compensation is unacceptable to Swat Pathans with any political ambition. A gift of money would do nothing to repair the damage to the personality; on the contrary, it would further emphasize the superiority of the murderers. Clients and tenants accept blood money; chiefs are forced, because of the importance of honour to their political career, to pursue revenge. In revenge, complete submission is sought from the opponent where possible. If that is not feasible, equality in retaliation is attempted, not as a principle of justice, but because such equality expresses the existing stalemate in power; it brings the feud to a halt by implying no loss of honour to either party.[1]

A particular kind of reputation is thus a valuable source of authority for a chief: a reputation for willingness to defend his honour and interests, for violence and impetuousness, for bravery and valour. The fact that a chief may do few of his revenge murders himself matters little in this connexion. As the responsibility falls on him who paid for the murder, it is he who requires the courage—the courage to live permanently under threat of revenge from an increasing number of people. This continual threat taxes his political skill and serves as a measure of his military power. Thus feuds in defence of honour become demonstrations of the relative abilities and powers of opponents; he who wins in such feuds and defends his honour thereby demonstrates his capacity as a powerful chief and competent leader. Little wonder that people admire him and that followers flock to his men's house; his reputation serves as protection to his followers as well as to himself. Little wonder, also, that leaders are driven to adopt this pattern in their relations with their rivals.

A chief who wishes to give way is subject to extreme pressures from his followers; if he does not defend his honour his reputation suffers, and his inaction is interpreted as a sign of weakness. His adversaries will inevitably

---

[1] Methods of settling feuds are discussed below, in connexion with the mediatory role of Saints.

press their advantage, to the detriment both of himself and his followers. Their interests are at stake as well as his, since his value as a protector is commensurate with his reputation as an avenger—and the risk is predominantly his, not theirs. Thus his own interests, and the expectations of his followers, as well as his personal self-esteem, all force him into the appropriate role of the status-conscious, honour-protecting, belligerent and ambitious leader.

THE PRINCIPLE OF OBLIGATORY PATRONAGE

None of the sources of authority so far described gives a chief command over any defined or exclusive group of persons. His tenants and other dependents emerge as a corporate group only if *he* mobilises them as such; they are held together only by virtue of their ties to him, and they are not prevented from having similar ties with other landlords. Similarly the recipients of a chief's gifts, or those who admire or fear him sufficiently to grant him authority, do not form delimited or exclusive groups. The political influence of a chief is amorphous, and its limits can only be ascertained when it is put to the test in particular conflicts.

Yet there does exist a basic framework of groups, in the form of the territorial organization (see Chapters 3 and 4). This defines a set of delimited and exclusive groups in the form of wards, ordered in a merging hierarchy of territorial subdivisions and divisions. Through the land tenure system, sovereign rights over these units are assigned, temporarily or permanently, to a corresponding hierarchy of Pakhtun descent groups. But the actual political authority of chiefs, deriving as it does from the several independent sources analysed above, is not contained within the framework of this hierarchy. In relation to the spatial framework, the net of political authority and dependence forms a pattern analogous to, but more complex than, that produced by the network of kinship in relation to the framework of a lineage system (Fortes, 1945, 1949). A chief may derive authority from several different sources over persons outside his own ward, and at the same time have no authority over many persons inside his ward. Yet the political power he derives from his control of followers, wherever they may reside, offers the basis for his position of influence and leadership within his ward. Wards and villages constitute administrative units, but the sources of political authority are to a considerable extent independent of such units.

The present section describes a principle of organization which creates some degree of congruence between the distribution of political authority and the territorial organization: namely, the principle of obligatory patronage. The system which results from this is known in Pashto as the *təlgeri* system, from *təl* = group, and *ger* = friend, associate. It formerly had a wider distribution, but appears always to have been adopted as a possible alternative only. Its underlying principle seems never to have been regarded as basic in Swat Pathan social structure. At present this system is characteristic of the Sebujni area of the Swat valley, and also, according to informants from that area, of the Karna valley in the Indus basin.

Stated simply, the system is based on a restriction of the contractual freedom of landowners in the employment of occupational specialists. Under the *talgeri* system, the landowners of a ward are obliged to give their occupational contracts to the smith, carpenter, barber, etc. of their own ward whom the chief of the ward has appointed.

As a result, the whole ward, not merely the estate of each individual landowner, emerges as a unit of production—duties are allotted and coordination enforced within the whole unit, since the various landowners must share a limited labour force, and depend on the same workshop and transport facilities. Similarly, by sharing a barber the members of a ward emerge as an association for the performance of *rites de passage*. Their community life naturally centres in the men's house, presided over by the chief of the ward, and the duties connected with its maintenance are distributed on some equitable principle between the members of the ward. The co-resident landlords of a ward are, as a result of the land tenure system, members of the same descent group as well as of the same caste, they have all their economic relations with the same group of villagers, belong to the same association for rites of passage and sit in the same men's house. The *talgeri* system creates congruence between the different analytically separate fields of commitment, producing a tightly knit, economically self-sufficient, and territorially compact and delimited community.

The main importance of this system lies in the way in which it affects the position of a chief vis-à-vis the other landlords of his ward. In the unrestricted system the various fields of commitment of any man cut across and disperse his loyalties and relations of dependence. A landowner may employ a blacksmith who is not a member of his own association for *rites de passage*, and he may sit in the men's house of a chief from another descent group than his own; while an agriculturalist may be the house tenant of one man, work in the fields of another, and possibly sit in the men's house of a third. Thus landowners come to have authority over some persons who are entirely free from any dependence on the chief to whom the landlord has declared his loyalty and a chief will have to share his authority over dependants with third parties, removed from his control. By the *talgeri* system these incongruities are eliminated. The chief of a ward will be the boss of its men's house and leading figure of its association for *rites de passage*; through these institutions he controls even those tenants and specialists whom he does not himself employ in their professional capacity. Through this control of the labour force of his fellow landowners, he gains a hold over them which he can never hope to have in the unrestricted system. The degree of authority which he normally has over the dependants of his own estate, and his own household, is in part extended to include the whole of the ward over which he presides, and he emerges as the leader of all the landowners of his ward.

As noted above, the *talgeri* system was formerly more widespread, but in the course of the last twenty years it has been abandoned in one area after another. The change has come about through meetings of all the chiefs of territories such as Babuzai, Nikbi khel, etc., at which they pledged themselves simultaneously to relax the restrictions which it involved. Thus the loss of authority to all chiefs was approximately proportional and simultaneous, and no single leader gained any advantage over his rivals. This move was in part initiated by the Ruler of Swat State; he brought pressure to bear on chiefs who resisted, and his support of the change made its implementation simpler. Today only the dominant leaders of Sebujni and Shamizai continue to impose the rule, whereas the chiefs of Thana, though they are subject to no control by the Ruler of Swat, do not do so. The change is thus not simply the result of a policy decision by the Ruler of Swat; the underlying factors are considerably more complex. As they pose a problem of historical nature, they can only be discussed briefly here.

Clearly the *talgeri* system is superior to the unrestricted system in providing for military defence. In the former, wards constitute unified, centrally led groups with the facilities of a men's house and, in former days, strategically situated fortified towers. In the latter, the alignment of neighbours in any conflict is not automatic, and the defence of the community does not rest unequivocally with a single unified group of men. With the increased security created by central rule in Swat and the Political Agent in Malakand, the importance of this military organization has diminished.

From the point of view of the Ruler of Swat, the advantages of the unrestricted system are obvious. It breaks up the solidarity of any grouping and guarantees the presence of established rivals for every position of leadership. Central control is maintained through the manipulation of such rivalries in the districts, and the system of unrestricted patronage considerably widens the scope for such intrigues, directed from the centre.

The point of view of the chiefs themselves, who after all have had the most significant part in implementing the change, is not clear. A relaxation of restrictions clearly leads to a reduction in the authority of chiefs vis-à-vis the outside world, and apparently also in a reduction of the degree of security of tenure in the position of chieftainship. But since attention is usually focused on *relative* position vis-à-vis similarly situated rivals, these considerations may be of secondary importance. A relaxation of restrictions does imply a greater freedom for the chief to decide policy. Under the *talgeri* system, his field of responsibility is pre-defined, and he is committed to maintain all members of his ward in his men's house, etc., lest they become discontented and pledge their loyalties to another pretender to leadership. In the unrestricted system, on the other hand, economy and efficiency may be maximized—a leader is freer to calculate the optimum size of his own following and maintain only such supporters as he sees fit.

He may slough off dependants at any time by dissolving his contractual ties with them; or again, when the need for more men arises, he may seek supporters wherever he chooses. There are limitations on such changes of policy, however; a leader who gets a reputation for fickleness has difficulty in creating a powerful and loyal following. Nevertheless the unrestricted system does allow greater freedom of manoeuvre.

The *talgeri* rule strengthens the position of the chief and somewhat simplifies the actual network of command and authority. It does not, however, affect the basic relationships between chiefs and followers.

GENERAL FORM OF A CHIEF'S FOLLOWING

In a political system one tends to think of the leader of a group as being the embodiment and representative of a corporate unit vis-à-vis outsiders. I have attempted to show that the Pakhtun chief in Swat is, rather, the nucleus around which form a corporate following and a field of political influence. I use the metaphor of a field to indicate the lack of definite limits, and the decline in the intensity of a chief's authority from a central group of dedicated supporters to the periphery of his following. This field of influence each political pretender must create for himself. The followings of chiefs are usually characterized by certain common formal features.

Very closely identified with the chief, and in every way dependent on him, are the members of his household: his sons, his estate overseer, and one or two intimate personal servants and bodyguards. These may owe allegiance to no other political leader. Though the sons may be allotted land to enable them to set up independent domestic units, the main body of a man's estate is never subdivided till after his death; and the political identification of sons with their father persists throughout the latter's life.

The bulk of a chief's supporters are formed by the regular occupants of his men's house: a solidary group of frequent associates, economically interdependent and largely dependent on the chief. Yet even among these there are considerable distinctions in the degree of their identification with the chief, and the kinds of sanction by which he can enforce his authority. These supporters include most of his land tenants and service contract holders (carpenters, muleteers, etc.), who are fearful of losing his patronage and also various persons who are heavily dependent on his hospitality for their sustenance. But there are also present many of his fellow landlords and descent group members who, though not as prosperous as himself, have rights over land and control dependents of their own. Their regular presence in the men's house is an expression of their political identification with the chief; but this identification is more like an alliance, even though not between equals, than a unilateral dominance relationship.

Outside this body of declared supporters, the chief has authority over many other persons. Invariably some of his land tenants and service contract holders prefer to dissociate themselves from political activity and stay away from the men's house—at the cost of the loss of its feasts and recreational facilities. Yet, through their economic association, they have some common interests with the chief, and he some sanctions over them; he expects to be able, if need be, to call on their support. Likewise, though some of his house tenants may stay away from his men's house, he has formal jurisdiction over them as his political clients, and holds the sanction of eviction. In areas where the *təlgeri* system of obligatory patronage is enforced, all these persons are concentrated in one ward and the chief's power to apply sanctions is thus somewhat enhanced; otherwise this system makes little difference to the form of his following.

Finally, in the fringes of a chief's field of influence are persons resident in his ward, but not in any direct relationship to him—e.g. the tenants of other landlords, who do not frequent his men's house. Through inter-mediate links, the chief is usually able to enforce his authority upon them; if not, he can in the last resort apply force or the threat of force to bring them into line.

Outside his ward and those immediately adjoining it, a chief will normally have very few dependants—maybe a few bribed agents, or business partners. He maintains numerous ties of alliance; but these give him no authority over persons in the sense of a right to command their obedience. Such relations will be discussed below (pp. 105ff).

Though there is generally one dominant chief in each ward, this need not be so outside the areas with a *təlgeri* system, and in many cases there are several chiefs in one ward. Thus one of the wards of Sangota in Babuzai is dominated by two chiefs who are not related to one another; and there are several chiefs in each of the large wards of Thana. In such cases, each dominant chief maintains his own men's house; only in one of the wards of Worejo in Nibki khel do two equal chiefs, paternal cousins, share a men's house—an exceptional case where political fission between collaterals has not yet taken place. A dominant chief must have his own men's house to enable his supporters to declare their allegiance to him. The support implied in sitting in a men's house is exclusive. A man may be the land tenant of several chiefs at once, or be the house tenant of one chief and sit in the men's house of another; but he cannot simultaneously be a member of two men's house groups. The men in a chief's men's house may have secondary ties, of a primarily economic nature, to other chiefs, and thus be to some extent subject to their authority; but their men's house identi-fication takes precedence in political matters.

Clearly, in this kind of system it is meaningless to look for a definition of 'the authority of a chief'. Chiefship in Swat is not an abstract office to be filled by a succession of incumbents. The authority of a chief depends, on the contrary, on the mandate he is able, at any given time, to wrest from each of his followers individually. This differs vastly in relation to his different followers. While he has—and many chiefs apparently utilize—the authority to command those who are completely dependent on him to make their daughters and wives available to him, he is unable even to criticize in public his near-equals among his following. The degree to which chiefs are able to command their following as a whole also differs greatly. This variation is reflected in the emphasis on conspicuous exhibition of the chief's power to command. Thus while I was visiting the men's house of an acquaintance in the company of a small group of chiefs, a former tenant of the chief, who had returned after a year's labour in the administered areas, came to pay his formal respects. He had invested a large part of his savings in an attractive wrist-watch, which he proudly exhibited. The chief stretched out his hand and took the watch, saying 'That will be your gift to me', and dismissed the man. He could undoubtedly have paid for a dozen such watches; the action was important mainly as a demonstration to all present of his complete control over his following.

The organization of villagers under chiefs in Swat is thus not an all-embracing system. Each chief establishes, as it were, a central island of authority, in the form of a men's house group, in a politically amorphous sea of villagers. From this centre his authority extends outwards with decreasing intensity. There may in fact be a zone of considerable autonomy —or overlap—between his field of authority and that of the next chief. In the traditional land re-allotment system such 'islands' were temporary, since the field of authority of each chief was built anew after every migration. With permanent settlement, there is a suggestion that the system is progressively consolidating; but this tendency, if indeed present, is obscured and counteracted by the rapid and frequent changes in the political fortunes of individual chiefs.

8

Authority and Following of Saints

THE SPECIAL STATUS of persons of holy descent and merit, and their relations to their disciples and followers, have been described above (pp. 56ff). In the present section we must consider such Saints in a wider setting, so as to understand the sources of their considerable political authority and influence. This description is complicated by the great variation in the kinds of community in which the status category of Saint is found, and the consequent variation in the social role of Saints. Prominent Saints, in part of the same descent lines, may be mystic recluses or minor landowners in villages ruled by chiefs; they may be headmen and rulers of villages which are held predominantly or exclusively by Saints but form enclaves within territories dominated by Pakhtun descent groups; or they may be political masters of whole territories. The Ruler of Swat himself belongs to this last category, and also makes considerable use of Saints in the higher echelons of his administration. Thus no simple description of the status of Saint can be given. Yet the category Saint has very definite social meanings; and the ways in which Saints in these different situations gain political influence, though modified by external circumstances, are basically similar. I shall therefore first describe these modes of gaining influence, and then discuss the differing form their political followings may take. The main sources of the political influence and authority of Saints are their control of land, their role as mediators and their reputation for morality and holiness.

CONTROL OF LAND

Most Saints own some land, and some are very prominent landowners. Title to land places the titleholder among the group of persons with a right to rule, and justifies him in actions as a politically autonomous person. It makes him economically independent of others, it absolves him from the onerous duties of a house tenant, and it also gives him authority over a group of economic dependants. It provides him with profits which he may use for political purposes. Finally, the distribution of the land owned by a Saint is such as to give him certain strategic advantages.

As has been explained (p. 66), land held by Saints (*siri*) is in a different category from that owned by Pakhtun descent groups (*daftar*). While *daftar* is traditionally subject to periodical re-allotment, and therefore gives the owner a right to speak in the public assemblies, which are concerned mainly with such allotments, *siri* belongs to its owner in perpetuity. The possession of such land gives its holder no right to speak in these assemblies. While title to *siri* land thus does not confer full rights of citizenship on its owner, it does, somewhat anomalously, give sovereignty over the land and those residing on it. On the basis of the usual house tenancy contracts, persons residing on a man's land become his political clients. In so far as he is a landlord, the Saint is thus forced into a political role: where Saints and Pakhtuns reside in one village, as is usually the case, the former, though debarred from the assemblies of landowners, must still act as patrons for their dependants. Seen from above, from the point of view of dominant descent groups and chiefs, the Saints are outside the political framework. But seen from below, Saints are the owners of fields and houses just like other landlords, and the person occupying a Saint's house requires and demands the kind of protection offered to the house tenants of Pakhtuns, since he himself can claim no political patronage from Pakhtun chiefs. Hence the political interests of a Saint, as well as his power to exert political influence, increase as his landed property increases.

A Saint may obtain land by inheritance, gift, purchase or conquest. The property of Saints is subject to the inheritance laws of Hanafi Islam with the modification that it can be held only by males. Sons share equally, and the presence of closer agnates excludes more distant ones. The amount of land which a Saint can expect to inherit thus depends on the size of his father's field and the number of brothers sharing. The inheritance rules can, however, be circumvented. Death-bed gifts are limited to one third of the total estate, but at any other time the owner, if of sound mind, has complete freedom to dispose of his property by gift. A not altogether uncommon practice among leading Saints is for the father in later life to make substantial gifts to his favourite son. Such gifts, among Saints, serve a function analogous to the *pargǝi siri* (see p. 75) of chiefs.

The usual way for a Saint to increase his landed property is by the receipt of gifts, particularly grants of land from Pakhtuns in return for his services as mediator. The settlement of major conflicts involving prominent chiefs, and thus large areas, is invariably concluded by a transfer of land to the peacemaker. In the traditional reallotment system, such transfers required the agreement, in a vast public assembly, of all the landowners with rights in the whole reallotment area of which the land in question formed a part. In spite of this difficulty, however, most of the land owned by Saints derives from such grants.

The Pakhtun re-allotment system also affects the location of the lands granted to Saints. Where, as among the Cyrenaica Bedouin (Evans-Pritchard, 1949), descent groups have fixed territories, there is a natural tendency for opposed groups, on re-establishing peace, to locate the grants to Saints along the border between them. Thus the mediator receives a compact area taken from the territory of both. This practice serves at the same time to create a buffer zone between groups with strained relations.

Such a location appears to be characteristic of the land grants given to the Sanusi in Cyrenaica. This leads Evans-Pritchard to conceive of the mediators as if they ' . . . in their lifetimes were regarded as standing outside the tribal system, to which indeed, being foreigners from the west, they did not belong . . .' (p. 67, see also p. 74). In the Pakhtun re-allotment system, quite other considerations carry weight, particularly the strategic advantages of different localities, the fertility of the soil, and relations with sedentary tenants. Accordingly, Saints are given land of inferior strategic value, difficult to defend, predominantly unirrigated or waterlogged areas, or fields at the terminal end of the irrigation channels; they are given the villages where the population is difficult to control, whether for topographic, economic or cultural reasons. These considerations are quite explicit, and are readily apparent in the distribution of Saints' lands in any area. The Pakhtuns try to maintain the approximate equality of their re-allotment units by equalizing the proportion of land alienated to Saints in each unit. Thus Saints' lands are dispersed throughout the different re-allotment areas of any one region. Saints and chiefs consequently co-exist in most local communities, and both form a part of local organization and community life.

A third way to acquire land is by purchase. This may serve to enlarge established holdings, but in view of the very high cost of land and the relatively weak economic position of most Saints, it is generally of little significance. Similarly, because they normally have only limited powers of coercion, and because of the restrictions imposed on them by the need to maintain a reputation for piety and justice, they cannot use the various violent techniques of land seizure practiced by chiefs.

Military conquest, though probably no longer feasible, has been of some importance as a means of acquiring land in the past. Most spectacular have been the conquests by prominent Saints such as Akhund Sadiq Baba and Mian Baqi Baba, eight to eleven generations removed from their present descendants, of land from the neighbouring Kohistani peoples as a phase of their conversion to Islam. These Saints led the Moslem armies against the Infidels, in their capacity as Holy men and leaders of *jihad* (see p. 60). But Islam is a political and legal as well as a moral and ritual creed; so the authority of the Saint to command the Army of the Faithful and convert the Kohistanis served also as authority to rule the conquered lands. Thus some branches of descendants of Akhund Sadiq Baba have maintained themselves as landowners in the Upper Swat valley, in territories around the villages of Madyan and Tirat (see Map 2, p. 15); other moderately large descent groups of Saints have established their control by similar means over the Alpuri area, and other villages on the Kohistan border in the Indus valley.

Such holy wars resulted in the creation of a belt of autonomous areas held by descent groups of Saints beyond the limits of the Pakhtun tribal lands; but minor military adventures at other times served to establish islands of Saintly supremacy within Pakhtun territory as well. The small automonous Saintly enclaves in the rugged hill areas were not all given as grants to successful peacemakers; some were simply seized. Pakhtuns themselves rarely reside in the small outlying hamlets on the ridges between valleys. Such villages are generally subject to remote control only, and form colony villages liable only for corvée labour (see the discussion of *sarkəli* villages, p. 45). These villages were particularly vulnerable to seizure by Saints.

For example, Parona and two small neighbouring villages in the Jambil valley of Babuzai territory were seized around 1900 by a small group of Saints tracing descent from Pir Baba (see p. 58). They had previously resided under the jurisdiction of Pakhtuns in the large village of Jambil; but relations with the dominant Pakhtuns there became more and more strained, and finally a quarrel led to violence. The leading Saint and his three brothers retreated, fighting, with their families, to three small hamlets higher up the valley but still within the territory of Jambil. There they built a central fort and several fortified towers, organized and armed a handful of resident tenants and herdsmen, and remained as squatters under constant siege. Some twenty years later, in the course of the conflicts surrounding the founding of Swat State, the Saints and the chiefs of Jambil both aligned with the Badshah, and a compromise was finally reached over the land, leaving the sons of the four brother Saints today in control of most of the land which their fathers had conquered.

By these various means Saints acquire rights to land and with them the responsibilities of landlords, and also sometimes political autonomy and supreme authority. The location and distribution of these land holdings have great implications for the political position of Saints. Thus, the leaders of the communities in the outer belt of conquered territories, such as that of the Akhund khel of the Upper Swat valley, are in a position essentially like that of a prominent Pakhtun chief. The headmen of village enclaves held by Saints within the territories of dominant Pakhtun lineages are in a roughly similar position, though more restricted in their field of manoeuvre since they are excluded from the assemblies of landowners. On the other hand their relation to dependants is permanent except in the Akhund Khel area, whereas that of Pakhtun landowners in the traditional re-allotment system is temporary.

A majority of Saints live as minor landowners in villages dominated by chiefs. But even in this case they are not entirely at a disadvantage. They may not speak in the assembly, but their title to fields is permanent. Their relations to all the villagers, whether their own dependants or the tenants and clients of others, are permanent and personal; their relations to inferiors are not subject to the periodical disturbance of re-allotment and migration. Even after thirty years of permanent settlement, this contrast is still readily felt; whereas the Pakhtuns live in the community as dominant strangers, the relations of Saints to fellow villagers has a pervasiveness which gives the Saint greater confidence and less need to affect his position.

Saints have a further advantage from the distribution of their lands. Pakhtuns have all their lands concentrated, at any one time, within one re-allotment unit, and usually all their houses in one ward only. Saints, on the other hand, are not contained by such boundaries, even where they live in wards dominated by Pakhtun chiefs. Their lands, and hence their dependants, are dispersed in areas dominated by different chiefs; thus they have some control over the followers of different leaders, and do not themselves depend on the good will of any one ward chief. Best of all, the advantages of this dispersal can be combined with those of auto- nomy. Thus the Nalkot Pacha, as well as being the headman of his own village, owns plots of land in various others, and so has a personal hold over some villagers in the men's houses of most of the neighbouring chiefs, while he himself is removed from the direct control of any one chief.[1] This control over dependants dispersed through several communities offers strategic advantages which the Saint is in a peculiarly fortunate position to exploit, as will be seen below.

MEDIATORS (*musipan*)

The status of Saints makes them particularly suited to the role of mediator or arbitrator. Though any respected person may play this role, Saints are generally preferred, and their functions in mediating in disputes have been conventionalized to such an extent that they are indispensable for certain standard procedures. Thus, for example, where the weaker party is no longer able to maintain a blood feud and wishes to offer his submission to his enemies and beg their pardon, the man most concerned must seek the assistance of a Saint. The two then choose an auspicious, or holy, night and proceed together to the home or men's house of the enemy. The Saint serves as a guarantee of free passage; without him the suppliant would be shot outright. He also serves as spokesman and explains the terms of sub- mission suggested. These would normally not include compensation, but almost invariably include a woman in marriage (*swara* = 'one coming on a horse', fem.) from the defeated to the victors. The chances of success depend on the persuasiveness of the Saint in pointing out the reasonable-

---

[1] A minor Saint in a small village controlled by Saints, whose economy and household I was permitted to study in exhaustive detail, holds the following land and thus has the following dependants in villages A–G:

A.   2 labourers, also his house tenants. He receives four fifths of the crop.
B.   2 tenants, also his house tenants. He receives two thirds of the crop.
C.   land cultivated by him assisted by corvée labour. He gets whole crop.
D.   1 tenant, for stipulated payment and corvée labour.
E.   1 house tenant.
F.   1 house tenant.
G.   2 tenants, for stipulated payment and corvée labour.

Of his nine dependants, only two live in his own village; the others serve to spread his influence, and his economic risks.

ness of the settlement, the advantages of peace, and the contribution of his magnaminity to the repute and honour of the victor.

Where a Saint is chosen as arbitrator in a conflict, the position is very similar. The opposed parties may agree to submit their case to arbitration, or the party that feels aggrieved may go to a Saint with their case, in the hope that his impartial verdict will strengthen their position and justify action by them, or force their opponent to compromise. The Saint must piece together the evidence and reconstruct the situation that led to the conflict and the actions of the persons involved.

We are not here concerned with the principles followed by Saints in reaching their decisions, except in so far as these have implications for their political position. In their role as mediators and peacemakers, Saints either speak on behalf of one party who is himself debarred from speaking, or they stand apart from and above the conflict, placing it in moral and legal perspective, and authoritatively apportioning guilt and responsibility. In both cases the party or parties who appoint the Saint by doing so surrender control of the conduct of their own affairs. Their relation to the Saint becomes temporarily one of complete dependence, since he holds their fate in the hollow of his hand. Furthermore, he has very considerable freedom in reaching his decision. He may settle the case by precedent or analogy from the holy texts—for holy law takes the form of cases and decisions, not that of a legal code—and he has considerable leeway in choosing the proper precedent or analogy. Or he may argue in terms of common Pathan notions of fairness and reasonableness, or by deceptively simple 'logical' principles of justice, such as equality. In other words, he is very frequently able, on the basis of the same facts, by choosing different ways of arriving at a settlement to reach widely different conclusions.[1]

On the other hand, the Saint has no institutionalized means of enforcing his decision. The parties to the dispute, though expected to submit to it, are under no effective compulsion to do so. The losing party, if it is the

---

[1] These two cases, illustrate these principles:

(1) Two brothers, A and B, claimed inheritance rights to the same field; A, in possession of the field, sold it to his paternal cousins. In retaliation, B seized one of A's fields. Verdict: B's action was wrong, because he did not take care that the area seized corresponded exactly to that of the disputed field. A's sale was invalid, since the brother, as closest agnate, was not given the first option. The three parties involved were called together to discuss a compromise.

(2) A man and his three sons lived together on an undivided estate. The sons all had families. One son died, leaving children. Later, the old man died, and his two surviving sons divided the estate. The orphaned grandson claimed his father's share. Verdict: by Koranic inheritance law, sons exclude grandsons from a share of the estate, the division between the two surviving sons was upheld.

In case (1), the actions of B were evaluated and condemned on the principle of fairness; he had acted in such a way as to profit from the conflict by seizing a larger field than that over which the dispute arose.

In case (2), a simple rule of holy law was invoked, regardless of its generally recognized unfortunate and unfair consequences.

stronger, in fact often refuses. In doing so, the leader of that party runs a certain risk, and he pays for his action by some loss of general support; he reveals himself as being an ungodly person, one not to be depended on. But the Saint as arbitrator can bring to bear on recalcitrants only such diffuse sanctions, and he has failed in this role unless both parties accept the settlement.

Against this background the political influence derived from the Saint's role as mediator can be analysed. The dilemma of the Saint is that he is in a position more or less to propose settlements in favour of either of the conflicting parties; but if his proposed settlement is not accepted, though this in no way reduces his religious merit and repute, it does immediately reduce his political influence. Chiefs and other pretenders value a Saint as an ally to the extent to which he works *for* them, and to the extent to which his decisions affect the situation. His political influence depends on the extent to which he can modify the actual course of any conflict or dispute, as judged by his past performance.

In making political capital of their role as peacemakers, Saints must thus take numerous variables into account and, in fact, be rather clever. This prevents few of them from trying. In the words of one prominent Saint: 'I look like a simple man; I live simply—but oh! the things I do!' The settlements which a Saint proposes must be justified by reference to some rule or ideal. They must also take cognizance of *de facto* situations, and the Saint must be skilled in inventing compromises and face-saving devices. As those who consult and appoint him are realists, he can also use the technique of 'passing the buck'. For example, one Saint's village lies very close to the border between Swat and Dir, and much of the political importance of its leader derives from his spiritual influence in the neighbouring Dir areas. When his settlements go in favour of parties in Dir, he can silence the Swatis by saying he must sometimes work against Swat, lest he lose his good repute among Diris. If within Swat one party feels wronged by his decisions, he can hint darkly that he only saved them from a worse fate at the hands of the Ruler or a prominent chief. If they are unconvinced by the logic of his verdict, he picks up his Koran and shouts: 'This is Islamic law, go and ask your mullah!' I have heard such techniques explicitly formulated and they are also exemplified in case material.

But without some force to back them, such manipulations sooner or later fall to the ground. The necessary force derives from several sources. Some of it is provided by the situation itself—where the Saint suggests a compromise between two more or less equally balanced parties, each is eager to defend *its* rights in the compromise. The consideration of the future value of the Saint's good will serves also as a coercive force. A man who has the good will of a Saint can, with fair confidence, appeal when needed to the impartiality of that Saint and expect him to do his best to arrange an advantageous settlement. And such good will is solicited by a public show of respect, and by submitting to the Saint's verdict where the cost is not too great. It is also won by outright support; a small chief not involved in a particular conflict may find it opportune to exert pressure in support of the settlement proposed by a Saint. In return for such favours he expects the Saint to exert himself on his behalf in later conflicts. The complementarity of the position of chiefs and Saints encourages this type of alliance between them.

But if the Saint himself disposes of some military power, however little, this greatly enlarges his field of manoeuvre. The Nalkot Pacha, my sometime host, was most explicit on the need to use 'both holy status and force'. His procedure is best illustrated by an example.

Two opposed persons from different communities were to meet with the Pacha on the border between the territories, so that he could make a settlement. One man came as instructed, alone and unarmed. The other brought a considerable armed party. The unarmed man sought cover behind the Pacha, the other party edged around them and were planning to execute the man before the Pacha, thereby forcing him to save face by pretending this had been his verdict, or else admit that he had been out-witted. But the Pacha put his fingers in his mouth and whistled, whereupon his own men, who had concealed themselves in the area several hours before the time set for the meeting, rose and converged on the breakers of the truce. These latter thereupon threw down their arms and begged the Pacha's forgiveness—so he settled the conflict on fair terms.

The small group of dependants controlled by a Saint *qua* landlord thus have an importance out of proportion to their numbers, since they can be used to second him in his special role as peacemaker. The control of land, and thus of dependants, involving as it does the self-interest of the Saint in the political intrigues of the community, might appear logically in-compatible with his role as impartial arbitrator. But in practical politics it is a tremendous advantage to Saintly mediators to control dependants.

Furthermore, we have seen how the lands of Saints are dispersed without particular reference to the borders between units in the land re-allotment system. Thus, while the dependants of a chief tend to be concentrated in his own ward and those immediately adjoining it, so that his political influence is contained within the segmentary hierarchy of re-allotment-units, the dependants of Saints are dispersed. Saints own much less land than chiefs and thus control far fewer dependants; but their channels of communication and influence extend much further. They spread their web of direct political influence over a much wider area. While the lands of chiefs help them to build a solid nucleus of control for purposes of administration and military dominance, the lands of Saints enable them to extend their influence over many communities, for purposes of arbitra-tion, mediation, the collection of information, and political intrigue.

REPUTATION FOR HOLINESS AND PIETY

The political authority of Saints derives also from the reputation for holiness and piety which they may gain by appropriate actions. Such a reputation constitutes an independent source of authority for Saints, as does honour for chiefs. This is most clearly shown in the case of the mystic recluses who are found occasionally in the Swat area. Without property of any kind, physically dependent on others rather than leaders of groups of dependants, and even without being active as mediators in actual conflicts, they are held in respect and awe by most villagers and in the course of time acquire very considerable influence. In the careers of politically prominent Saints, this reputation frequently precedes other factors as a source of their authority. Thus the Akhund of Swat, descended from a subject ethnic group in Bajaur and himself a goatherd, arrived on the political scene without property and without influence in 1816, and settled in Beki, a village on the bank of the Indus. There 'he secluded himself continuously for twelve years and devotedly prayed to God night and day, taking only herbs. When he attained the purity of soul, his magnetical spiritual powers had reached far and wide. In short time thousands became his disciples . . .' (Zabeeh, 1954, p. 5). A reputation for piety is thus not merely conceptually separate from other aspects of Saintly status, or a reflection of authority gained from other sources. It is a separate aspect of a Saint's position, evaluated separately by Pathan villagers, and in itself sufficient as a foundation for a claim to political authority.[1]

A Saint's reputation in terms of performance is evaluated by criteria quite different from those applied to chiefs. Many acts which would bring honour to a chief, such as the immoderate display of violence, would be regarded as most inappropriate in a Saint, and might seriously harm his reputation.

It would be meaningless to characterize a Saint as *nar saṛei*, 'a virile man'—a common term of approval for chiefs. Similarly, to use its opposite *khaze*, 'woman', of a chief is a serious insult, but if applied to a Saint the word is irrelevant, or in a sense states the obvious.

---

[1] Not all, needless to say, are as successful as was the Akhund. A Saintly mystic, calling himself *Pir*, was at the time of my fieldwork attempting to set himself up in a village in the mountains. According to one disciple 'he isolated himself and fasted, but accepted pupils; many local villagers started coming to him. Once a mad Gujar herdsman came, but the other pupils objected that he was filthy and wanted to send him away. But the Pir answered that he must bring such persons also to the right path, and he gave the herdsman lessons. Once while the herdsman was asleep in the forest the shadows of spirits fell upon him, he rose from his sleep quite changed, did strange things, vomited, and could no more speak Pashto, only spirit language. But the Pir understands him and has now converted him to a perfect religious man, eagerly pursuing knowledge.' This competition the established local Saint finds somewhat inconvenient; his comments throw some light on the relations between the two of them: 'The Pir came from Peshawar District some twelve years ago, and became honoured for his pious actions; his wife was also venerated by women. He gave a couple of daughters to the local chiefs; then his wife died, and he wanted a daughter of the chief to replace her. But one of the young men of the family ran off with that girl—they were in love. So now there sits the Pir, starving himself and talking spirit talk to the loony old Gujar.'

Truly 'Saintly' behaviour implies moderation, piety, indifference to physical pleasure, and withdrawal from the petty and sordid aspects of common life; and also wisdom, knowledge, and the control of mystical forces. Thus Saints tend to move quietly and speak softly, but with dignity; they prefer immaculate white dress, carefully observe all the ritual rules of ablution, and prayer, and practise fasting and other abstentions beyond those enjoined on all Moslems. The Badshah, for example, since he retired from active government of his State, fasts the whole year round, from before sunrise till sunset. The excesses of chiefs have no place in this style of behaviour. Even hospitality is not emphasized. A saint must give freely to the needy, but tends to give little at a time; so in common parlance *Mian sarei*, 'Saintly fellow', is often used in the sense of 'miser'.

The awe in which Saints are held by the villagers, is derived from their knowledge and mystic powers. Most people firmly believe that if they were to kill a Saint, misfortune would befall them and they would themselves probably die. This awe is enhanced by the isolation of most Saints; they do not partake in the daily life of the men's houses, or in the more ribald community amusements associated with weddings, holidays, etc. Finally, they are believed in varying degree to control mystic and miraculous powers, revealed by their ability to cure many diseases, write amulets, and so on. Denials by Saints—some of them fiercely orthodox—that they possess these special powers merely enhance their reputation. In terms of the mystic and esoteric ideas of Swat Pathans, such denials are only evidence of the great piety of the Saint. Holy things should not be disclosed. This principle of the proper concealment of miraculous powers was illustrated to me by the following story:

In the days of the Akhund of Swat, or Saidu Baba, many pilgrims came to see him and pursue knowledge under his guidance. One man came from Syria; it took him eleven years to get to Swat. He spent the day with Saidu Baba, then confided in him that he had made a pact with his wife in Syria that if he did not return after eleven years, she should be free to remarry. He now had only one night left; it would take him another eleven years to get home the way he had come, his wife would have remarried and his life would be ruined. So Saidu Baba instructed him to shut his eyes, place his foot on Saidu Baba's foot, hold on to Saidu Baba's shoulder, and not open his eyes till Saidu Baba said he might. The moment he shut his eyes, he was miraculously transported to Syria; he opened them and saw before him his wife and mother. So he decided to migrate with his whole family to Saidu to live with such a wonderful Saint. When he arrived for the second time in Saidu, Saidu Baba made him promise never to tell about the miracle, and to suppress his ambitions. This he did, and he settled down and lived a pious life.

By appropriate acts and demeanour, Saints may thus enhance their reputation for holiness. This reputation gives their opinions great weight, particularly among the more pious or gullible sections of the population, and thus contributes to their political influence. Utilizing such a reputation, a verbally facile Saint can very profoundly influence community opinion, both among the body of villagers, by setting them up against the dominant landlords, and among the landlords themselves, by changing their point of view or threatening them with accusations of heterodoxy. The Badshah of Swat, himself a Saint, clearly realized the political importance of such authority, and the essential unpredictability of Saints without vested land interests, who rely for authority only on their reputation. His first action on having established himself as Ruler was therefore to expel, as politically undesirable, all Saints and mystics who did not own property.

THE GENERAL FORM OF A SAINT'S FOLLOWING

Deriving from the general principles of village organization in Swat, and particularly from the three sources discussed above, the political authority of Saints of some prominence may be seen to be compound, and may conveniently be described as extending over a series of concentric zones.

The nucleus of a Saint's political following consists of his close agnatic relatives and his dependants. Saints emphasize seniority somewhat more strongly than do Pakhtuns; thus, in a group of brothers and paternal cousins, the senior man is usually the political head and has authority over the others. Through land tenancy and house tenancy contracts, the senior Saint also gains authority over a small group of dependants, of tenant or craftsman caste, who reside on or earn their livelihood from the fields belonging to the small descent group of which he is the head. As pointed out above, this small number of political followers are generally dispersed, so that the Saint has authority over members of numerous local communities.

The next wider zone of political authority and influence embraces the whole area over which this primary group of dependents are dispersed, which again is co-terminous with the area in which the Saint is regularly active as arbitrator and peacemaker. Within this area are also concentrated most of his disciples, i.e. those persons with whom he maintains permanent relations, who seek his advice in matters of ritual, morality and politics, pay him formal visits at the time of religious festivals, etc. Relations with the more prominent Pakhtuns in this area are often reinforced by marriage; thus the line of the Nalkot Pacha is related to the chiefs of Sebujni, in whose territory Nalkot forms an enclave, as shown in Figure 7.

Such affinal ties serve to intensify social contacts through joint participation in associations for *rites de passage*, and exchanges of visits. In this wider zone the area in which one Saint is active may overlap that of another, so that in some villages or districts several prominent Saints may be rivals in authority and influence. The more prominent Saints are generally active in a larger area. Thus Miangul Abdul Wahdood, later Badshah of Swat, had, before the creation of the State, property and interests throughout the Swat valley, well outside the territory of the present State.

Finally, the reputation of a Saint reaches beyond the area within which he is regularly active. It defines the widest limits of his influence and also represents his field for potential expansion. It is his reputation for holiness and piety which attracts new followers, and leads to his being nominated as peacemaker and arbitrator in areas which were formerly outside his

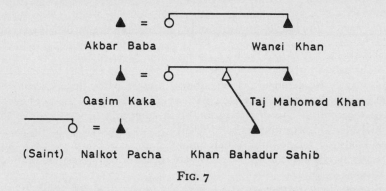

FIG. 7

field of authority. This reputation also reaches more generally through the population of his own area, and lends authority to his disciples and dependants when they act or speak on his behalf vis-à-vis persons with whom he has no direct relations.

As a political leader, a Saint exercises influence and authority in all three concentric zones; but their relative importance varies according to the structure of the larger community of which he is a member. In areas where large descent groups of Saints hold sovereignty over autonomous areas, the inner central core of direct control over economic and political dependants becomes vastly expanded, and the wider zones of influence have secondary importance only. In such cases, the structure of the Saint's following is essentially similar to that of a chief. Where Saints reside together with Pakhtuns in a territory, their reliance on the second zone of authority, as advisers to a larger group of disciples, friends, and affines becomes more in evidence. But this authority continues none the less to depend on the presence of a central core of dependants. Finally, where such direct control over a nucleus of dependants is lacking, Saints are forced to rely on the third zone of authority, maintained by reputation only.

9
Alliances and Political Blocs

THIS DESCRIPTION of the political system of Swat has taken the form of a progressive synthesis of component parts, leading in the last two chapters to an analysis of the formation around leaders of politically corporate followings. The second main step in the synthesis remains: that of showing how the combination or opposition of these smaller groups creates the actual political organization of the valley. This requires a description of the kinds of relationship which imply mutual political support, and conversely, the kinds of structural situation that imply opposition between leaders.

The striking feature of the political organization of Swat is the emphasis on free choice and contract which is fundamental to the organization on lower levels, and also characterizes the wider political alignments. Thus the political organization does not derive directly from any one of the frameworks of organization previously described; it is a distinctive framework of its own, based on a series of explicitly political contracts or alliances. Yet these political alignments clearly are not formed without reference to the other social facts, and to analyse the organization one must look at the way in which such facts affect the choices that are made.

In other words, the description so far has shown how there is, on the one hand, a formal and embracing framework of organization based on territory and descent, and, on the other, a multiplicity of small nuclei of political control, represented by individual political leaders and their followings. A group consisting of a leader and his following is politically corporate in the sense that it acts as a unit for political purposes.

I shall now describe the political organization that develops from the activity of these groups within the formal framework defined by the system of territorial and descent units and their associated hierarchy of public assemblies. Empirically, one finds that the many smaller corporate groups are aligned in two grand dispersed political divisions or blocs (sing.: dəla).[1] This fusion into two blocs results from the conclusion of a series of alliances between leaders of the smaller groups. Each bloc contains members from nearly every local community, and includes Saints as well as chiefs among its leaders. Our purpose here then is to describe how the

[1] I am indebted to Martin Southwold for suggesting to me the term *bloc* for these groups.

blocs are formed, their political functions, and the way in which certain structural features of the territorial and descent frameworks are reflected in their composition.

The basic bond on which this wider organization depends is the alliance. An alliance between two political leaders in Swat is a contractual agreement that the two will support one another in the defence of their several interests; it is a contract of political fusion in opposition to outsiders. A leader is free to establish such an agreement with any person: he is not compelled to give political support to any person—though he is expected to be loyal to his father and full brothers—nor is he committed to oppose any particular person or group, as he would in a true moiety organization. The kinds of alignment analysed in the preceding chapters are between persons fundamentally unequal in one or several respects, and the political solidarity which they imply derives from shared interests in a joint enterprise and from the control of sanctions by the leader over his dependants. The solidarity of the alliance analysed here springs from a different source. The partners in an alliance are, *qua* political leaders, essentially equal, and they are not engaged in any other joint co-operative effort, nor is one able to bring particular sanctions to bear on the other. Their solidarity derives from the mutual strategic advantage they obtain from the relationship; if this advantage disappears in the eyes of one or both partners, there are no external constraints to prevent them from repudiating the relationship and thereby terminating the alliance. In other words, an alliance in Swat is a political contract.

The significant feature of this relationship is the degree to which political alliance is conceptually distinguished from all other contexts of association and common interest. Political solidarity between equals is not an implicit aspect of any other relationship, such as common descent or kinship, common membership in a congregation, territorial propinquity, etc. It is a separate subject of contractual agreement and thus of free individual choice. Other principles of organization are relevant only in that they are considered by the individuals when they make their choice. Some such principles have great strategic implications and thus affect the kinds of choice that individuals will tend to make, as will be shown below. But no other principle of organization is structurally identified with the relationship of political alliance.

A second feature is the lack of relativity that characterizes relations of alliance and opposition in the Swat political organization. In societies with a highly segmentary organization—and Swat seems in many respects to belong to this type—we are accustomed to find a system of continual political fusion and fission, whereby groups unite in opposition to an outside threat, but break apart in opposition over internal conflicts. (Evans-Pritchard in Fortes and Evans-Pritchard, 1940, pp. 281-4.) This pattern is not characteristic of the alliances of Swat. Though there is rivalry between individuals within an alliance, this is kept in hand. An ally is an ally in any situation, regardless of whom he opposes. It is inconceivable for a leader, without repudiating an alliance, to be opposed to a person in one situation and allied to him in another. This will become clear from the nature of the commitments implied in an alliance.

The relationship of alliance is a contractual promise of mutual support in political conflicts, particularly relating to debates in public assemblies and to the use of force. A man whose material rights or privileges are threatened calls on his allies; and they are committed to support him by using their influence to protect his interests and make his opponents abandon their claims. If unsuccessful in this, they must support him by force of arms—as he must likewise support them if their rights are threatened. Before the establishment of State organization in the upper valley, and still today in the lower valley, all military operations other than holy wars were carried out by these alliances. Within the present area of the State, the Army and the Police Force represent the physically most powerful organizations. But it is still true that no larger locally based groups than the bloc of allies emerge as corporate units in the use of force. Thus, if two persons start fighting over a field, it is, outside the body of their dependent followers, their respective allies, and not their fellow villagers or their lineage mates, who rally to their support. Likewise, in debates at public assemblies a man's allies are committed to support him, and allies co-ordinate their efforts with a view to the tactical advantage of the group as a whole.

Conflicts in defence of honour fall outside the field of alliance. A state of *pokhto*, conflict involving blood revenge, is a personal matter and does not involve the larger corporate alliances; it obtains essentially between individuals, and a man's honour can only be defended by his own might (see p. 82).

Alliance groups can meet in opposition on a considerable scale, in the public assemblies that govern regions of 30,000 inhabitants, and in battles involving thousands of soldiers. Furthermore, tension between them, though variable in intensity, is nearly always present to some extent in all areas; every community has its unsettled conflicts and ancient grudges. The alliances, then, are not formed *ad hoc*, but persist, and the contracts between members which constitute them are of fairly long standing. Thus they must necessarily be systematized; a man cannot simultaneously pledge support to two allies who are aligned on opposite sides. The value of the alliance to its partners lies precisely in the compulsion on each to support the other in every situation. In cases of divided loyalties, one alliance or the other must be repudiated. In this way, because of the wide radius of communication and participation and the considerable pace of political activity and intensity of opposition, the consistency of alignment and opposition is maintained within regions. Furthermore, the blocs of neighbouring regions pair off, so that a pervasive two-party system emerges, extending through the length and breadth of the Yusufzai area.

The blocs thus persist through time, as continuing corporate groups, and form the main framework of political organization.

The formalities of establishing or repudiating an alliance are simple, but public. An alliance is established—usually after careful secret negotiations—by a public declaration, generally accompanied by a joint meal. Thus, when the position of the unpopular, but dominant, chief of Barat khel, Babuzai, crumbled because of events affecting his prominent allies outside the Barat khel area, all but two landowners of the four Barat khel villages abandoned him and transferred their alliances to his rival, Rashid Khan of Odigram. This was made public by a joint meal, consisting of tea and hard-boiled eggs, with all the minor leaders, in the course of which Rashid Khan declared his willingness to protect their interests, and they their willingness to support him. A repudiation is even simpler: the seceding leader sends one of his servants to the men's house of the locally dominant leader of his former alliance, and from the gate the servant shouts 'My master repudiates the alliance' (*māta kṛi* = lit.: broken he-makes), and then runs.

An intimate and firm relationship of alliance is generally accompanied by frequent visiting and dining, joint hunting and fishing trips, etc., as well as by the necessary meetings for purposes of discussing tactics, and by corporate action on appropriate occasions. Frequently such bonds are reinforced by inter-marriage, both between the households of the leaders themselves, and between their close personal followers. Thus my friend Aurangzeb Khan of Mingora, himself a SiSo of his now deceased close ally in Worejo, Nikbi khel, arranged in the course of my stay for the marriage of his servant's son with the daughter of one of the Khan of Worejo's faithful retainers, and the two chiefs combined to beat down the brideprice to a level where the boy's family could afford the union.

The giving of a woman is in itself a major gesture of friendship. Furthermore, the affinal tie creates opportunities for frequent social interaction through joint participation in associations for *rites de passage*. However, there is nothing to prevent marriages taking place between persons of opposed groups, so long as they are not at the moment engaged in war, and there is no unrevenged murder between the two families. At any one moment, there is no obvious correlation between affinal ties and ties of alliance, but the affinal ties with allies occasion more intensive social interaction. If it were feasible, however, to correlate intermarriages with political alliances at the time when the marriages were contracted, I strongly suspect there would be a significant positive correlation.

TENSIONS REFLECTED IN THE DISTRIBUTION OF TIES OF ALLIANCE

The alliances which combine to produce a system of two opposed blocs are designed by the contracting parties to ensure a position of strength vis-à-vis rivals and enemies. The pattern of alignment of persons is thus best understood as a mirror image of the pattern of structural tensions between persons. The natural allies of a man are those with whom he is not in competition. A brief reminder of the sources of the power and authority of leaders will serve to show which persons are rivals, and which are potential allies.

The potential authority of chiefs and other Pakhtuns derives predominantly from the control of land (see Chapter 7). Through land they gain control over house tenants, occupational contract holders and land tenants, and other dependants; while from it they reap the profits which enable them to enlarge their followings by giving feasts and gifts in their men's houses. Furthermore, chiefs gain authority by defending their honour, particularly through blood revenge; but this activity is largely a personal matter and falls outside the field of alliance. The conflicts into which allies are called for support are almost always conflicts over land or crops. They concern rights to land, the borders of fields, rights to irrigation water, damage to crops, division at inheritance and division at the periodic re-allotments. When considered in conjunction with the rules of land tenure, it becomes apparent that conflicts of this type must produce tensions between certain specific categories of social persons. Conflicts over the borders of fields, rights to irrigation water and damage to crops inevitably arise between neighbours, while conflicts over rights to land, inheritance and division at periodic re-allotments must arise between collateral agnates.

A re-examination of the land tenure system shows that owners of neighbouring fields and collateral agnates tend to be the same individuals. The traditional re-allotments followed the segmentary scheme of unilineal descent. Regions were allocated to large descent groups and their primary segments divided between them the areas in that region. Their component secondary segments in turn subdivided each area (see pp. 65-8), and each secondary segment then divided the villages of its sub-area between its component segments. Thus, depending upon the size of the village and the number of shares held by the Pakhtuns in question, a village might be held by ten to a hundred separate landowners, related by a patrilineal genealogy of five to ten generations' depth.

However, in the case of the largest villages the land area of the village was usually permanently split up into sub-units, as for example the ward divisions of Thana, so the ultimate group of landowners dividing the fields of one compact area between themselves seems to have ranged between ten and forty.[1] This group of ten to forty agnatic collaterals thus become perennial neighbours, in spite of periodic migrations. Since the last major

[1] The following villages, in each case divided into two wards, are held by the following numbers of independent Pakhtun landowners:
Sangota (Babuzai) by 7; Worejo (Nikbi khel) by 26 (4 of dominant lineage); Biha (Sebujni) by 38 (34 of dominant lineage); while one of the four main wards (Baba khel ward) of the giant village of Thana (pop. 10,000) has sixteen independent Pakhtun (Baba khel) landowners (see genealogy of Thana, pp. 26, 27).

re-allotment, which took place in most areas about thirty years ago, such groups of agnates have become established as permanent owners of the land in a fixed area with an extreme dispersal of holdings due to attempts at the time of settlement to equalize the value of the land equivalent of each share. Thus neighbours with whom conflicts over the borders of fields, irrigation water, etc. arise, are today and have always been also one's collateral agnates, with whom conflicts over succession and re-allotment arise.

One aspect of the traditional re-allotment system deserves to be emphasized, since the conflicts and cleavages of today—and thus also the alignments in the party system—are coloured by conditions in the recent past. The re-allotments between large groups generally concerned areas of approximately equal value. These were assigned to groups in rotation, or by the drawing of lots; and the periodic re-allotment created no great conflicts between the social units so opposed. At this level, trouble might be caused by the condition of the vacated buildings, or of the fields and irrigation system. It was usual to remove the roof-beams on departure, and instead of manuring the fields during the last year of residence, to transfer the accumulated manure to the new fields. As long as these practices were adopted by all, they did not give rise to conflicts between the alternating groups.

The final stage of the division, that of village lands between individuals, however, did introduce sources of conflict. Individual shares differed greatly in size, and the village lands were not permanently divided into the particular configuration of shares existing at the moment of re-allotment. Each new settlement had to be negotiated afresh, the equivalence of different fields argued and balanced up, access to irrigation, other economic considerations and strategic factors weighed against each other. The very principles on which the land tenure system was based thus inevitably produced acute tensions within the small group of sharing collateral agnates. Even permanent settlement within Swat State has not altogether eliminated this tension, since river-bank rice-lands continue to be held on temporary tenure.

This tension inherent in the relationship of agnatic collaterals is clearly recognized by Pathans. Such opposition is in no way regarded as ideal, for loyalty to one's agnates is a great virtue, but rather as one of the regrettable facts of life. Pathan kinship terminology uniquely distinguishes agnatic collaterals from all other cognates in ego's generation. In the parental generation, Fa (*plār*), FaBr (*trə*), MoBr (*māma*), Mo (*mōr*) and FaSi = MoSi (*trōr*) are distinguished, and the terms are extended to classificatory siblings of parents. In ego's own generation siblings, cross cousins, and MoSichildren are all classified together as Br (*wrōr*) and Si (*khōr*), while FaBrchildren, real and classificatory, are distinguished by a special term (*tarbur*). This term further has the connotation of rival, enemy (Morgenstierne, 1927), and is not used as a term of address except as an insult or challenge.

Within each community, then, the strongest tensions develop between landowning agnatic collaterals. This prevents the descent groups from fusing for political purposes. It serves to direct the Pakhtun's political attachments to non-rivals in neighbouring communities. These attachments take the form of the alliances described above; through them the Pakhtun tries to secure protection from, or dominance over, his local agnatic rivals.

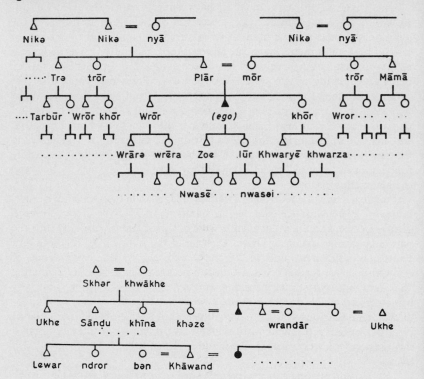

FIG. 8. Consanguineal and affinal terms in Swat Pashto.

A person manipulating the alliances strives to build up within his local area a majority directed against his rivals. The majority in this case is not measured in numbers of landowners, but in effective power, which depends on the total number of active supporters which the coalition commands; this is roughly proportionate to the total area of land which it controls. Because of their numerical and military superiority, Pakhtun chiefs tend to dominate the blocs; but Saints with their followings constitute particularly useful members of any bloc because of their special role and privileges and their powerful influence among the lower strata of the population.

The Alignment of Leaders in Blocs

For the tensions between collateral agnates to be perfectly mirrored in the actual composition of local blocs, there would have to be political fission of every line in every generation. As sons succeed their fathers, the estates of brothers descend into the hands of cousins. Pathans, in my experience, often talk as if this necessarily resulted in splitting the political unit formerly represented by these estates. But the factors described above produce only tension, not actual fission; and the tensions outlined may be counter-balanced by other forces. They obviously have no effect on the alignment of individuals until they are made manifest in overt action. There are, in fact, important strategic and other considerations which tend to delay their overt expression. Thus persons whose structural position implies rivalry may continue together in alliance for a considerable length of time. Swat Pathans use the term *māriz* for persons who are local rivals but nevertheless belong to the same bloc.

In the first place the mere fact of group opposition is a deterrent to fission. As the trusted agents of their fathers, young men are active in politics long before they become established as independent landowners; and in the course of this period they establish wide contacts with their father's allies. Their friends tend to belong to his bloc, their enemies to the other (see Appendix, case 2, for the connexion between politics and youth groups). Even when considerable differences develop between two collaterals within one bloc, neither is particularly anxious to abandon all his established friends and join the enemy. The leaders of the bloc are similarly concerned to prevent secession, and exert all their influence to hold the group together.[1] Much of the political activity of prominent leaders is directly concerned with arranging settlements and compromises between groups of allies.

Another deterrent to fission is the necessity of belonging to a politically viable unit. As will be shown in some detail below, local blocs develop a co-ordinated strategy in arriving at compromises with their opponents, giving concessions in one dispute in return for gains in another. The solidarity of each bloc is based on the strategic advantages which the members gain from mutual support. For a landowner to hold his own within his own bloc he must be strong enough for his support to be of

[1] Thus, when my friend Aurangzeb Khan heard of the death of the Khan of Worejo village, he immediately travelled to Worejo with a dozen of his allies and important dependants. Though in different regions (Nikbi khel and Babuzai respectively), the two Khans were closely tied by political alliance. The village of Worejo, though divided into two wards, was in fact completely dominated by the Khan, a senior member of the Manki khel segment, who are less numerous but far richer than the Shado khel segment, and thus able to control Shado khel ward as well as their own. In case of fission within the Manki khel, Aurangzeb Khan would be embroiled, and half the village lost to him as allies in any case. He therefore spent in all several weeks effecting a settlement and supervising the division of the inheritance in detail.

value to the other members, lest they simply seize his land, or make him carry the brunt of concessions to the other side. Thus, while wealthy sibling groups—or even individuals—can stand alone because they control a large force of dependants, small landowners must combine to secure the necessary strength for independent political action. If they fail in this, they cannot be anyone's allies but must be someone's dependants (*Khān pa lās ke*=in the hand of the chief). Tension between collaterals is thus kept within bounds by the tactical advantage of presenting a solid front to outsiders. In general, therefore, among the smaller landowers the politically unified descent segments are large. In such areas as the Upper Sebujni or Jinki khel, where Pakhtuns form a third or even half the population, and the average holding of land, and following of tenants, is correspondingly smaller, fairly large Pakhtun descent groups remain politically united; whereas fission frequently occurs between first cousins or even half-brothers in the lower parts of the valley, such as Thana and parts of Babuzai, where Pakhtuns number less than one tenth of the population.

Nevertheless the tensions between collaterals do ultimately lead to fission; and the very persistence of a system of two opposed blocs requires such a process to be operative within descent lines. To show this, a number of interdependent processes need to be considered. The ways in which the more powerful landowners encroach on the property of the weaker have been outlined. The result is a continual sloughing-off process, whereby Pakhtuns who lose all their land forfeit their Pakhtun status. But for this, the rapid growth of population among landowners (see p. 79) would lead to the fragmentation of estates and progressive impoverishment of the Pakhtun caste. In fact, the evidence indicates that in the present century the sloughing-off process has more than offset the natural growth of the Pakhtun population and that land has been progressively concentrated in fewer lines and fewer hands.

These processes relate directly to the constitution and fission of blocs. In any local area, one or other alliance will at any given moment be dominant. It will constantly exert pressure on the members of the other, which will thus suffer continual losses. The stronger are not interested in increasing their power by concluding alliances with members of the opposite bloc. They already dominate the area, and take advantage of their position, not to solicit alliances, but to wrest land from members of the weaker bloc. Accordingly, in the course of time the weaker bloc shrinks, firstly.in the number of its Pakhtun members (since those who lose all their land lose their Pakhtun status), and secondly and more rapidly in the total area of land, and so the total force of men, that it controls.

If no other factor intervened, this would lead ultimately to the elimination of the weaker bloc. In fact, both blocs continue to exist because there are secessions from the stronger to the weaker. As the majority bloc grows increasingly powerful, political rivalries will develop within it. This rivalry is encouraged by its opponents, and finally one of the subsidiary leaders of

the stronger group is enticed to go over to the other side and become its
leader. In this way they gain the military superiority, and the tables are
turned. The rivalries within the dominant bloc which lead to such secessions
are regularly between close agnatic collaterals. Thus the tensions explored
above find their direct expression within the framework set by the strategy
of the alliance system.

These processes are illustrated by the recent history of the chiefs of
Maruf khel, Babuzai, as given by numerous informants of both blocs.
These chiefs have attained a level of wealth where fission is possible even
within sibling groups.

The opposition in this area in the last century was between Malak Baba
of Maruf khel and the chief of Juna khel. Malak Baba nearly exterminated
the Juna khel, establishing himself as leader of the dominant bloc and
meanwhile increasing his private property from four to fifty shares (*Rupəi*)
of land. Upon his death, disagreement over succession and inheritance led
to fission between his sons. Nowsherawan Kaka succeeded his father, and
Jamroz Khan seceded from the bloc with his full brothers, his half brother
Janes Kaka, and all their followers, to join the remains of the Juna khel
and become their leader. There was, incidentally, never an ordered
division of the estate of Malak Baba. Each group of sons seized the fields
in the area controlled by their party; but at the subsequent re-allotments
each brother had a legal right to one eleventh of the father's fifty shares.
Jamroz Khan joined an alliance with the Mianguls (the Badshah, later
founder of Swat State, and his brother Shirin Sahib, see p. 35) and his
party dominated the Babuzai area; but when the Badshah and Shirin
Sahib later became estranged, Jamroz Khan supported the latter, whereas
the party of the former, supported by Nowsherawan Kaka, came into
power. Shirin Sahib was later killed in battle. Later on, as Nowsherawan
Kaka's bloc grew in strength and threatened to become independent of
Badshah's support, the latter abandoned him and joined the other bloc.
They arranged the murder of Jamroz Khan, supporting Pir Mohammed
Khan (Jamroz Khan's half-brother's son) as the local leader of their bloc.
This led to a split between Pir Mohammed Khan and the sons of Jamroz
Khan and his full brothers, who broke away under Aurangzeb Khan.
The two surviving landowners of any importance in Juna khel today,
though rivals, remain together in one group because of these cross-cutting
enmities.

Unilineal descent, through its relevance to succession and land holding,
thus affects the composition of political groups; but it does so by causing
rivalry to develop between related persons, not by defining bonds of solidarity
and co-operation. Such bonds are indeed defined, and are significant for
example in revenge; but the structural opposition of the interests of
agnatic collaterals prevents their fusion as a solidary political body, and
leads to this pattern of alignment in opposed blocs.

Finally, one other aspect of the situation needs to be made explicit: the persistence of factions within each bloc. Though the overriding opposition is *between* the two blocs, tensions produce clearly visible lines of potential fission *within* them. The local rivalries between *mariz* (see p. 111) are only one example among many. Alignments are in general unstable; factions develop around rival pretenders to leadership, not exclusively between close agnates. Thus in the example just given, opposition persisted within the bloc between Jamroz Khan and the remnants of Juna khel. But such opposition does not lead to violence—except when it leads to a new alignment—and does not take place in public, as does that between blocs which are openly opposed.

THE ORGANIZATIONAL SIGNIFICANCE OF ALLIANCES

The political leaders of an area, with their followers, are thus grouped through a set of alliances into two opposed blocs. The leaders of each are the chiefs and other powerful landowners, each the leader of his own men's house. A number of minor landowners align themselves with these leaders through regular association in a men's house, either as respected, though weaker, allies, or as *de facto* dependants. More intimately tied to the chief are the followers, mostly not landowners, who serve as his retainers and agents. The main force at the bloc's disposal is composed of the large body of tenants and craftsmen who congregate in the leaders' men's houses, who reside in the houses owned by the landowners of the bloc, and who serve these landowners on various contracts. In case of actual battle, the control of this large body of men becomes crucial; until such a point is reached, however, their participation in politics is negligible. They all, however, require the protection of the bloc. This the leader can offer by virtue of his superior wealth and command of a co-ordinated body of followers. Without such protection, his individual followers cannot defend their property and their lives. Finally, Saints or colonies of Saints, with their followings, are incorporated through informal alliances to be discussed later.

The cleavage between the two blocs looms large in the daily life of the community. Most male life is centred in the men's house, with its exclusive one-party membership; and the boundaries of neighbourhood groups are generally those of wards or their subdivisions, dominated by a single leader and committed to one bloc. If such a neighbourhood unit is a division of a ward, its members attempt to erect a separate mosque for one-party worship.

The importance of the blocs in group life is strikingly exhibited in connexion with witchcraft beliefs. According to the theory applied by most anthropologists, accusations and suspicions are directed against persons with whom relations of dependence and competition exist simultaneously (Marwick, 1952). Pathan witchcraft beliefs take the form of fear of the evil eye (*nazer*), believed to embody power, often unknown to its possessor, to cause harm through envy. According to the explicit statements of all informants, corroborated by recorded cases, only the evil eye of allies and members of one's own bloc is dangerous.

PUBLIC ASSEMBLIES

The effects of the cleavage between blocs thus extends through most fields of daily activity. But a group wider than the membership of a single men's house is rarely mobilized as a corporate body. The chief significance of the wider organization is in the fields of government and politics. Particularly in the meetings of the public assemblies, or *jirgas*, the local blocs emerge, through their representatives, as co-ordinated and corporate bodies of the greatest importance.

The hierarchy of public assemblies of landowners is characteristic only of the acephalous Pakhtun-held areas of Swat. The governing assemblies of areas controlled by Saints are much more informal. Within Swat State, the importance of assemblies has steadily declined since the State was founded. The following description therefore refers directly to the area outside the present borders of the State, exemplified by Thana. But all the evidence indicates that the system there is that which was common to all the Pakhtun areas of Swat up to the nineteen-twenties.

Some general features of this system have been mentioned above (pp. 67ff). Each re-allotment unit is governed by a public assembly of the landowners in a Pakhtun descent segment. In practice the most important of these are the assemblies of one large village or a group of smaller villages, such as Thana in Lower Swat, Balol Khel in Sebujni; or Barat Khel in Babuzai.

The assemblies provide an institutionalized setting for meetings between the two opposed local blocs. But before the role which these play in the assemblies can be described, the rules governing the assemblies themselves must be summarized. Some of these rules are highly formalized, and have a profound effect on the tactics of the opposing parties. They relate mainly to the right to speak, the procedure for summoning the assembly, and the rules of procedure.

The right to speak in the assembly is confined to patrilineal descendants of the apical ancestors in terms of whom membership is defined, who hold land in their own name, or in other words, to the heads of Pakhtun households of the descent group concerned. Thus, in the assembly of Thana, all landowners descended from Amza, Kanda or Ali have the right to speak, as they are the heads of the Pakhtun households of the Thana re-allotment area (see figures). In the more limited assembly of Bazid khel, only the landowning descendants of Amza may speak; while for larger regional assemblies, the main groups within Thana each send several representatives. The important feature of this rule is that no landowning household head of the appropriate descent group may be denied the right to argue in the assembly, no matter how small his share of land. To ensure this, the person of a member is sacrosanct while he is on the assembly meeting grounds; but this does not imply that there is a general free conduct to the place, and in fact members have often enough been prevented by threats or force from reaching it.

The assemblies do not meet at regular intervals. Either some member calls a meeting, or all agree at one session on the time of the next. Any member may summon the assembly to discuss any subject—though in fact only the major leaders of a bloc do so without consultation. The village or small area assemblies, which meet frequently, employ one or two permanent servants (*kotwāl*, or *jirga nāzer*) who are not themselves members, and whose duty is to notify the members of meetings, and to collect fines payable to the *jirga* as a body. For their services they receive an agreed quantity of grain each year, which is contributed by the members in proportion to their holdings of land. Where no such regular service has been instituted, the individual landowners use their own barbers for this purpose.

There is no fixed quorum. All landowners need not be present; on the other hand, decisions are regarded as more binding on those who were present than on those who were not. As the assembly rarely initiates action, and serves primarily as a forum for negotiation, this fact is of slight importance, and its decision in each case is based on a realistic evaluation of the extent to which those present truly represent the interests concerned.

The meeting itself follows certain set rules of procedure. All members of the assembly sit in a regular circle on the ground in an open public place, often in the shadow of a large tree. These rules are considered by Pathans to express the underlying principles on which the *jirga* is based. No man must sit higher than any other, on a bed or a stool, because all are equal as *jirga* members. Similarly the circular seating, by the same logic as King Arthur's round table, eliminates precedence and thus expresses the equivalence of members. The meeting place itself should not be the property of any one member; and an uncultivated place, in winter sometimes a mosque, is accordingly selected.

A speaker who wishes to have the attention of the assembly stands up; otherwise the debate does not appear to an observer to be subject to any particular regulation. As there is no chairman, persons often speak at once, while members converse freely with their neighbour on any topic of interest. Thus, though every member has the right to speak, this does not mean that everyone will listen to him, and in the middle of his speech another may rise and start discussing another aspect of the problem. Throughout the meeting there is much coming and going. Members call allies and opponents aside for consultation and bargaining; and the course of the debate seems to a considerable extent to be determined by such lobbying.

The final decision of the assembly should be unanimous. This is not ascertained by a vote of any kind, but by the absence of open opposition. Needless to say, this allows considerable room for manoeuvre to both parties. Most decisions are in the form of settlements of disputes. The person in whose favour the decision goes is authorized by it to act in self-help within the limits specified by the settlement. No member of the assembly is committed to help him in this—though his allies will normally be ready to do so, as they thereby inflict a loss on the opposed bloc. On the other hand, as parties to the decision, all members are committed to refrain from resisting him in obtaining his right. Thus, while a man who wins a case is usually assured of help from his allies, the other bloc has, through the assembly decision, withdrawn its support from the loser. He therefore stands alone, and is rarely in a position to resist.

Occasionally, decisions of other types are made as well. Contempt of the *jirga* and damage to public property (roads, major irrigation channels, pastures) are punished by fines collected by its servant or other delegate. The rules of procedure are upheld by the pressure of the bloc opposed to the person who breaks them. Public works, particularly those involved in the irrigation system, are sometimes initiated. Each landowner generally contributes labourers in proportion to his area of land, or in matters of irrigation in proportion to the area which will benefit from the work. But such joint activity is inevitably difficult to arrange, since landowners profit to different extents from any one irrigation channel, so that new works affect the balance of power between established factions. As a result even necessary repairs may be neglected, and land fall into disuse, as some of the fields of Thana have, because of political complications. Where electric power is available, some chiefs use wells and electric pumps for irrigation water, in spite of the considerably greater cost, expressly so as to avoid these complications.

The difficulties which arise in activities which are objectively to the general advantage and to nobody's detriment, reveal the fundamental structure of the assembly. It is not, as one might have believed, the governmental body of a politically corporate group; it represents an institutionalized mechanism for arbitration between opposed landowners or blocs of landowners. For this reason the presence or absence of this particular mechanism—as we shall see in the discussion of Swat State—does not greatly affect the political system.

The way in which the assemblies function, most characteristically in the settlement of disputes, may best be illustrated from an actual case. The names used are fictitious.

An assembly met in a Swat village to consider a conflict over the exact location of the border between fields of the estate of Nawab Khan, and those of a dependant of Abdul Khan. In other words, it concerned the right to a narrow strip of land between these two properties. It was agreed that Nawab Khan had once owned the land; he became addicted to opium and finally died from the excessive use of various narcotics. Abdul Khan's ally started using the field, claiming he had obtained the right to it from Nawab. Rashid Khan, who was Nawab's FaFaBrSo and the guardian of his two younger brothers, became aware of this after a couple of years, and brought the case before the assembly. Rashid Khan was at the time an ally of Rahman Khan, while Abdul Khan was one of the leaders of the other bloc in the village. Neither bloc completely dominated the area.

Rashid Khan opened the meeting by stating his case in detail, calling on several members to support his evidence on specific points. Abdul Khan led the defence, questioning the evidence and trying to mobilize evidence for his man's case. This led to a considerable amount of talk, and numerous speakers, often several at once, debated matters marginal to the case. Meanwhile Rashid Khan consulted, behind a nearby haystack, with various prominent chiefs, first his own allies (including, for example, Abdul Khan's younger brother), then members of the opposed bloc. Rahman Khan's brother, whom Rashid Khan had supported closely within the bloc, but not followed when he went over to the other bloc, apparently promised not to use his influence one way or the other. Ultimately Amir Khan, whose influence had recently been growing within his bloc at the expense of Abdul Khan, promised to support Rashid Khan in return for certain concessions in another matter. Abdul Khan then changed his tactics and began attacking Rashid Khan, saying, 'We must not always listen to this Rashid Khan, and do all he says in all matters—we are not his dependants. Here the other day he got his way in that irrigation dispute, now he wants to decide who shall own land.' Whenever the main leaders spoke, the other members listened; otherwise there was a steady murmur of conversation. However, Abdul Khan's attack did not arouse much response and the hum of conversation started rising; so he knew that he would lose his case. A Pakhtun rose to support Rashid Khan. Abdul Khan told him to be quiet and not contradict his betters. At this Rashid Khan's party became furious. Rahman Khan shouted through the din, 'Is this a common street-brawl? Who says a member of the assembly may not speak against this or any other Khan?' He and Rashid Khan rose and left the meeting in protest, followed by their party. Rashid Khan's bloc brought a case against Abdul Khan for contempt of the assembly; but he had effectively prevented them from coming to a decision on the disputed field. His ally—who would eventually be made to cover the expense of Abdul Khan's fine—thus remained in possession of the field for an indefinite period, at least till the assembly again got around to discussing the case.

Such tactical manoeuvres, designed to protect the interests of allies and the strength of the bloc as a whole, are characteristic of assembly activities; and specialized skill in such manoeuvres is a highly valued attribute of leaders. This constant emphasis on the interests and advantage of allies prevents us from regarding the assemblies as governing bodies, and analysing the extent of their authority and the field of their activity. The empirical facts force us to give primary attention to the organization into blocs and the principles of rivalry and balanced opposition on which this organization is based, and to regard the assembly meetings as merely one institutionalized field in which these principles are expressed.

Opposition between Blocs

The main framework of political organization in Swat is thus given by the alliance series. The two local blocs formed by these alliances form corporate groups,[1] though with relatively rapidly changing membership. These politically corporate groups do not, however, pursue consistent policies over long periods. They are mobilized only in opposition to other similar groups, or rather to any political body which threatens their interests. This opposition may take several forms. It may, as we have seen, emerge in the forum of the public assembly where Pakhtun members of both blocs meet in debate, and the balance between the two is decided by the force which each represents, and the apparent determination of each to apply this force in defence of their respective claims.

Alternatively one or both blocs may mobilize a body of men in a show of force, to bring matters to a head so a settlement may be negotiated, either through the assembly or, more commonly, through an arbitrator, or may actually take up arms, and meet in battle in a real test of force.

Nowadays, in the Swat valley, battles are rarely fought, though they appear to be common in the neighbouring Dir and Bajaur. Hence this method can only receive summary treatment. The alternative procedure, however, deserves fuller description, particularly as it illustrates the kind of relationship that is established between chiefs and Saints in the alliance system.

Show of Force

An encroachment on a man's rights, or an obvious threat to them, usually leads to the mobilization of a group of his allies. This takes the form of a declaration, in some public idiom, of the loyalty of allies and dependants of the person whose interests are directly threatened. Through this affirmation of support, a dispute between individuals becomes converted to a dispute between blocs. Invariably, this involves the massing of men in a show of force, since only through such concentration are the blocs able to act. In the case of a localized dispute, this show of force may take place on or by the object of dispute.

In one village where I worked, when an old disagreement flared up over the boundary between two fields, the rival leaders at an agreed time lined up their local party along the disputed border. These party members included all castes: tenants, herdsmen, craftsmen, and the private servants of the chiefs, as well as the other landowners of the community. If there is great discrepancy between the forces, the weaker party must give in. If they are moderately evenly balanced, a mediator (*musipan*), usually a Saint,

---

[1] i.e. they persist through time, they act as units in a co-ordinated fashion, they have an internal distribution of authority and responsibility, and they exist explicitly to protect a joint 'estate' in the form of the sum of the rights and privileges of all the constituting members. This is not affected by the fact that the bloc may be divided by internal factionalism.

is appointed. In the present case, however, fighting broke out. One Khan's father had been shot by this same rival leader in a skirmish over the same field fifteen years earlier, so that feeling ran high. The two parties had agreed to meet without firearms; but once they started fighting, using sticks and stones, members of each party ran back to the village to fetch arms.

Where the disputes are not strictly localized, or involve a larger community, the show of force takes place at the men's houses of the leaders involved. For example, a Khan was insulted by his enemy. Within an hour allies began to congregate in the men's house of his leader (his first cousin). This group of landowners was at the time under heavy pressure from the dominant party, and they felt that their enemies would take advantage of any temporary weakness or involvement on their part. To forestall this, all their party supporters in the town where the events took place made a public demonstration of their numbers and loyalty. Each and every ally made a visit to the men's house of the leader (there being a great number of men's houses, of both blocs, in the town), some to stay for a long time, others to sit merely for twenty or thirty minutes as a demonstration of their loyalty. At no time during the day did there seem to be fewer than forty men in the men's house; at times there were more than a hundred. The retainers of the Khans kept close watch on who made an appearance and who did not. As above, both landowners and groups of clients joined in the demonstration. Word of this massing in the men's house spread, as usual, like wildfire through the bazaar and very quickly reached me at the opposite end of the town; and the movements of key leaders were widely known and discussed.

The mobilization of local sections of both blocs in opposition by a show of force, leading to a concentration of members of each in an excitable, heavily armed group, may, as in the first example, lead to actual armed conflict. But the purpose of the operation is the mobilization itself, as a preliminary not to battle but to negotiation from a position of strength. The leaders of the blocs almost inevitably speak in favour of compromise; and such counsels generally prevail in the Swat valley today. Contact is then established between the two opposed groups, generally by the naming of a mediator; and the parties submit to a truce, usually maintaining the *status quo* with respect to the object of conflict pending a settlement. Such a settlement is then generally negotiated by the mediator—either a local Saint or, in Swat State today, a Tahsildar or Hakim of the State, who incidentally is often a Saint by descent.

In their attempts to settle such conflicts, Saints are themselves embroiled, not so much in the specific disputes of individuals as in the tactical manoeuvres concerned with the balance of power. However, since the traditional functions of Saints are being progressively taken over by the State organization, my material on this point is defective, and I can do no more than sketch certain aspects of the traditional situation.

The fact that the various Saints are regarded as allies of specific Pakhtun leaders is however clear. For example, the two opposed blocs in the Babuzai area were known at the beginning of the century by the names of their respective leading Saints, of the villages of Ser and Sardarei. Similar explicit alignments were found in every area in which I worked. The way in which both chiefs and Saints profit from such alliances has been indicated (p. 98). The Saint, to be politically successful, needs military support on a considerable scale, and this a chief is in the best position to provide, while the chief profits from the good will of the adjudicating Saint. The followings of these two kinds of leaders can, moreover, overlap. While a man can be a member of one men's house group only, religious tutelage to a Saint is not a violation of the obligations owed to a chief.

The importance of the tie between Saint and chief is increased by the political importance of conflicts, over and above the particular matters in dispute. This might be expected from the following considerations. The characteristic lability of political groupings among Pathans clearly springs from the nature of the following of chiefs. In a leader's career defeats as well as successes tend to become cumulative. A defeat, for himself or one of his followers, reduces the chief's field of influence, his marginal followers leave him, his rivals increase their pressure, and unless this process is quickly checked, further defeats follow in an accelerating series. Inversely, successes swell a chief's following and lead to further successes. The outcome of any conflict even of apparently minor importance, may tip the scales between two rivals and quickly lead to a succession of defeats or victories. Therefore, a conflict which has been brought to a head by the mobilization of allies in a show of force requires a settlement which takes the pattern of alliances, as well as the facts of the particular dispute, into account.

This was clearly realized by the Heir to the State in his settlement of a case in which an insult was avenged by an important Khan's followers. The successful avengers were fined by the Heir; but simultaneously he stated in a public audience that the Khan and his brothers were his 'mamagan' (uncles—actually FaFaBrWiBrSo.s), and that any insult to them was an insult to him, thus inhibiting further action by either bloc of allies.

Minor Saints of Swat are obviously less powerful and more dependent in their relations to the chiefs between whom they try to mediate; they cannot dictate their terms, and are forced to take sides in the opposition as members of blocs, so as not to be reduced to mere pawns in the hands of powerful chiefs. Thus, for example, the Akhund of Swat, by completely committing himself to one set of alliances, e.g. by public prayers for the success of his allies, gained a strong position and finally complete control of the whole bloc.

But because of their particular role, requiring a certain minimum of 'impartiality', Saints are not as closely tied by their alliances as are Pakhtuns.

Thus Nalkot Pacha for example, can permit himself to criticize and even give judgements against the wishes of Khan Bahadur Sahib, the leader of his bloc. The bond of alliance is thus looser between Pakhtun and Saint than between two Pakhtuns. The formal criterion of the political alignment of Saints which is used most frequently by Pathans is thus not so much their judgement of cases as their ceremonial visits at the time of the main calendrical festivals.

USE OF FORCE ($jang$ = battle)

Conflict, a show of force, and settlement outside the public assemblies thus serve to mobilize whole local blocs, rather than their leaders only, and also bring Saints into the bloc organization. The body of men who assemble for a show of force are in fact the same who fight together in battle. Fighting on any considerable scale, such as flared up almost continuously at the beginning of the century, is now rare in Swat. Apart from minor skirmishes in small villages, quickly stopped by the intervention of the Ruler of Swat or arbitration by the Political Agent in Malakand, the last case of war was in 1949 in Batkhela (pop. 6,000 to 8,000) in the Lower Swat valley. It arose from a case of blood revenge which got out of hand when the pursuers tried to force an entry into a men's house where the pursued was hiding. Allies joined in on both sides and fought through the day. Dependents from the outlying smaller villages poured in and joined the fighting, but it did not spread outside Batkhela.

Fighting between blocs is classified as *jang*, battle, and death in battle does not call for revenge. From the circumstances of any situation it is usually possible to distinguish between murders committed by rivals, which cause shame and can only be wiped out by revenge (see p. 82), and death in battle, which is honourable and in no way a matter of shame for the deceased or his descendants. Accordingly struggles between blocs, though they lead to violence and death, do not take the form of blood feuds; and the tie of alliance is one of mutual support in politics, not one of shared jural responsibility in blood revenge.

In the case of the other most recent conflicts—the *jihād* in Kashmir, when perhaps ten thousand Swatis took part, and a fairly recent massing of forces on the Dir-Swat border—the units mobilized were not political blocs, and at least titular leadership was held by a single person. The striking feature of wars between blocs of allies, on the other hand, is the lack of co-ordination which has usually characterized them. This lack of centralization has both technical and political implications.

Perhaps because of the widely shared understanding of military tactics among leaders and followers alike, Pathans have apparently been able to unite in effective military action without any clear hierarchy of command. The most striking example of this from the Swat valley is that described by Churchill (1898), when a force estimated at twenty thousand besieged the newly established forts at Malakand and Chakdarra and involved the

Indian army in a major operation. The campaign was initiated by an inspired priest (among Pathans widely recognized as insane), but was in no way led by him; yet the tactical requirements of the operation were apparently effectively met by the Pathan force. In this case, as in that of battles between alliance blocs, many organized groups of men, each under its own leader, formed units in the larger army; and the necessary co-ordination was achieved informally by councils of leaders of groups. The point which deserves emphasis is that the tactical requirements of co-ordination in battle can be satisfied, even in the case of very large forces, without the development of any formal organization of command and hierarchy among the leaders.

RESULTANT FORM OF ORGANIZATION

The group of allies in any area develop only as much co-ordinating organization as they need to be able to unite in the particular kinds of situation to which the alliances are relevant. From the above description, certain common features of these situations are apparent. In all three main types of situation a bloc which is called into action congregates in one spot. Debates in the public assemblies develop along unpredictable lines, and only those present are able to participate in the decisions taken. A show of force in the men's house consists precisely in the massing of allies and their dependants in one place, and only by visits to men's houses are the bonds of alliance confirmed. Finally, in the case of battle, allies draw their men together to fight as one unit. As a consequence, the alliance blocs are only activated in response to particular issues—they are called together to act with reference to each specific threat, but are otherwise inactive, as their members are dispersed through a wider territory.

No circumstances require the members of a bloc to delegate authority to any one leader, since every time the group emerges in action its members are able to consult one another. Furthermore, the success of the bloc depends precisely on its elasticity and ability to respond quickly by changes of tactics to changes in the situation. Consequently, the blocs do not develop any permanent administrative organization, and are unable to pursue any long-term policy.

The bloc thus retains an acephalous organization, the units within which are groups of men each with its own leader, most commonly men's house groups. Each alliance between two such leaders forms a link in a wider network, and because of the large groups of allies that are occasionally mobilized, these networks become systematized into a pattern of opposition between two main blocs in every area. Pathans therefore conceive of their organisation as a pervasive two-party system. But in fact the systematization extends no further than the largest units which are mobilized. For most purposes these maximal units are the blocs within the regions of the traditional re-allotment system such as Nikbi khel, Babuzai, or Sebujni. But such units are never clearly separated. Leaders form alliances across the borders of regions, such as that between Aurangzeb Khan of Babuzai and Worejo Khan of Nikbi khel (p. 107). Such alliances are of no use for debates in the public assemblies, since the partners never participate in the same assembly meetings; but in cases of battle or the show of force they are of considerable value. Each bloc within any region is thus to some extent linked with one or other bloc in the neighbouring region. There are also occasions when the blocs of several whole regions are mobilized simultaneously. Formerly there was large-scale fighting which could spread through the whole upper valley; and today the relations between prominent chiefs and the Ruler of Swat lead to the emergence of wider alliances. These very prominent leaders, by spreading their net of alliances very wide, thus create some degree of consistency in the alignment of local blocs in opposition. But this does not affect the fundamental character of the organization. The wider links are inoperative in most situations, and the regions within which opposition is significant are the sub-areas within each region.

THE POSITION OF LEADERS IN THE BLOCS

Each bloc is, then, an acephalous organization of a number of individual political leaders, supporting each other against the opposed bloc. But each such leader is the leader of a centralized political grouping—for Saints a group of disciples, centring around a mosque, for chiefs a men's house group. Thus, though the wider organization is acephalous, it is made up of units of fair size, each with its centralized internal organization. While the blocs have no continuous corporate existence and do not pursue long-term policies, there is nothing to prevent individual leaders from pursuing such policies. Indeed, most of them are compelled by the pressure of circumstances to attempt to enlarge the unit under their control so as to provide followers with spoils.

From the point of view of any individual leader, he is in the centre of a series of concentric circles. He is first and foremost a member of a particular village, which contains his main rivals and, unless it is a very small community, also several other leaders, some allied to him and some to his rivals. Within his local re-allotment area he is a member of a bloc composed of many leaders, some stronger, some weaker than himself. His rivals belong to the opposed bloc. Finally, he and other members of his bloc may have ties with prominent leaders in neighbouring areas.

Most leaders are Pakhtun chiefs and so preside in a men's house which is continuously occupied by members of their following. While the larger bloc to which a leader belongs emerges as a group only occasionally, he has an organized group permanently in existence in his men's house. He seeks to use the alliance organization to his own advantage. If he is a leader of some prominence he may dominate the bloc within his village, in which case he is in a position to mobilize it frequently and thus increase his influence. Until he attains considerable power, however, he does not control the larger bloc of allies within a wider area, among them he is subject to a majority swayed by the most powerful leaders. It is this outer sphere of his own bloc which holds the key to his success. Every time he can cause the larger bloc to be mobilized in matters connected with himself and his followers, or resist its mobilization for purposes not directly to his advantage, he has succeeded in gaining more from the alliances than he has given. Thus, by judiciously allowing or preventing the mobilization of his own bloc, and finally by seceding at the opportune moment, a leader may gain advantages at every turn, regardless of the successes or failures of his allies. The restrictions on the growth of a bloc, and the rough balance that obtains between such blocs in any one area do not imply corresponding restrictions on the development of the power of individuals. The case of Malak Baba (see p. 113) is an example.

Such growth in the power and property of a leader logically implies the political centralization of his followers. Yet, though centralized Khanates have developed elsewhere they have not appeared in the main Swat area. This has not been for want of pretenders, but is the effect of various disruptive forces.

The obvious disruption factors are the equal division of property between sons, the pattern of personal revenge, the difference in the rate of increase of supporters and opponents, and the opposition of other leaders to the acquisition of predominant power by any individual.

As has been observed (p. 79), wealthy landowners tend to have large families. The presence of many sons is a considerable asset while their father is alive. The group composed of a man and his sons, in contrast to any other in Swat society, has complete community of interests, since their joint estate remains undivided and any increment will be to everybody's advantage. Such a group can co-operate in an unusually effective fashion; and Pathans regard it almost as a prerequisite of political and economic success to have many sons. Anyone who succeeds in considerably enlarging his estate, and thus the total political unit under his control, generally does so with the support of his sons; but at death a man's estate is divided equally between his sons, so that large estates tend to be split up in every generation. Where a leader becomes prominent enough to have land in several villages, he establishes a separate household in each, occupied by a wife and her sons. For example, Khan Bahadur Sahib of Sebujni has houses and men's houses in three different villages of lower Sebujni. He himself occupies the different houses in turn, and thus binds them together as one political demesne; on his death, the sons will succeed in their separate villages and the political unit will break apart.

To increase the area of land under his control at any appreciable rate, a political leader must use violence or the threat of it. In pursuance of such ends Jamroz Khan's younger brother and main instrument, Amir Nawab Khan, reputedly killed forty-one men by his own hand. Such killings call for blood revenge, so that the extension of a man's estate inevitably creates a steadily mounting number of persons dedicated to wreak vengeance on him. Amir Khan was himself killed, and his estate divided between his three sons. Thus the more rapidly a man increases his estate and thereby the centralized group under his control, the greater the chance that his career will be cut short.

In the segmentary organization, a leader trying to expand the group of persons directly under his control creates opponents more rapidly than he creates supporters. By the alliance system he can extend his influence widely within his own bloc. But to achieve centralized control a man cannot use the bonds of alliance, since they imply equality; he must use the bonds of clientage. He must therefore seize land. After extending control over most of the land of his own minimal descent group, he turns his attention to his nearest collaterals. With sons and luck and force of character he may be successful in ousting one group from their lands, in the course of which some of them are killed, and others go into exile in neighbouring villages. If he then attempts to go further, and tries seizing the land of a more distant collateral group, itself divided into opposing blocs, he merely succeeds in uniting them against himself, as any member of it has a stronger claim than his upon the land in question. Needless to say, if he attacks members of a more distant collateral descent group, the group which he thus unites in opposition to himself is all the greater. By seeking to expand into their lands, he forces a re-alignment in the alliance blocs. Though his land area, and the force of tenants he controls, is increased, he has lost allies, and the outcome is a net increase in the number of his opponents. Moreover, his disinherited enemies will oppose him with far greater fervour than his adherents—tenants and clients who must be won by gifts—will support him. Some of the prominent Khans of Swat are caught today in this very difficult position.

Finally, other leaders follow such trends and are both jealous and afraid of one who is too successful. Their remedy is to support some rival for his position. Once he has been reduced, support may be withdrawn from his rival too, and balance in the acephalous bloc system thus be restored. This strategy is implicit in the support given by some Pakhtun chiefs to rival Saints (e.g. p. 100, n,), and in the support to Shirin Sahib against his brother the Badshah (below, p. 128).

This brief summary brings out the main factors inhibiting the growth of centralized units. No single strategy of expansion can be designed to overcome these difficulties. Thus any expanding centralized unit within the acephalous alliance system must experience strains which eventually lead to its dissolution.

10

History and Organization of Swat State

CHAPTER 9 described the acephalous political organization of Swat as it actually exists today in the part of the valley included in the protected tribal area of Malakand. In spite of these factors which militate against centralization, a native State emerged in the period between 1917 and 1926, and has become firmly established in the upper two thirds of the valley. This was achieved by a different strategy from that discussed so far, namely by seeking influence rather than possession of land. The founder of the State did not draw his power only from the sources described above; he also developed a new kind of relationship between himself and a number of individual contract-holders, who were organized to serve as his army. A full analysis of this development falls outside the scope of the present work; but certain aspects of it will be summarized. I shall try to show in brief outline how Swat State was formed within the pre-existing political framework, and how its organization in part uses that framework.

The chronicle of events in the Swat valley may be read simply as an example of the actual functioning of the political system described above. I hope to show how the processes I have described are still fundamental to the political constitution of Swat State. Above all, the maintenance of social order still depends very largely on the bloc organization.

Attempts by prominent leaders to establish domination over all Swat appear to have been made throughout the period for which historical records are available (see Bellew, 1862; Wylly, 1912, 111ff). The Akhund of Swat exerted great influence, and for a while supported Sayyid Akbar of Sitana (leader of the *Mujahidin*, p. 62) as the secular leader of a confederacy of tribes. On the Akhund's death, Ramatullah Khan of Dir began to extend his sphere of influence into Swat, while the Akhund's senior son, Abdul Manan, became leader of the opposed bloc. On the latter's death, his brother and his two sons joined opposing blocs; at the same time Omara Khan of Jandul succeeded in expelling the Nawab of Dir and established a strong centralized rule in that area, until he was defeated by the British after his invasion of Chitral in 1895 (Robertson, 1899). The Nawab was reinstated and paid considerable subsidies by the British; he began to levy irregular taxes from the tribes on the west bank of the Swat River, while the political leaders in Swat remained unable to unite in resistance.

Abdul Wahdud,[1] son of the Akhund's junior son, began to build up his position as soon as he came of age. First he induced his cousin Amir Badshah to leave the bloc of the latter's brother, Sayyid Badshah. Later, in 1903, Amir Badshah killed his brother; but shortly afterwards, he was himself killed. Abdul Wahdud, Badshah, became sole heir to the property and position of his grandfather, and a prominent political leader.

His bloc in the Babuzai region was dominated by the Mian of Sardarei (p. 121) who had become extremely powerful and ruled most of the small valleys between Swat and the Indus, though not the main one, which was always dominated by Pakhtun chiefs. By seceding from that bloc and joining the Mian of Ser, the Badshah shifted control over the area to the other local bloc and simultaneously gained dominance within it.

The tribes of Swat finally combined in a confederacy against the Nawab of Dir, but elected as their head Sayyid Abdul Jabbar Shah, grandson of the former leader Akbar Shah. However, the Badshah and the Sandakei Mullah, who was active in Swat at the time, united as holy leaders and denounced Abdul Jabbar Shah as a heretic, as he was connected with the Qadiani sect. After a year or two they were able to raise a rebellion against him. Later he established himself in a tiny feudal state in the tribal area by the Indus.

Immediately after the rout of Abdul Jabbar Shah the coalition broke up, and the Badshah and the Sandakei Mullah became rival pretenders to leadership. The latter was supported by the Taj Mohammed Khan of Sebujni among others (p. 71), the Badshah by the Darmei Khans of Shamizai and the Khans of Babuzai. The Badshah's supporters drove the Sandakei Mullah out of Swat, in spite of an alliance he had formed with the Nawab of Dir. After the victory, Badshah was elected Ruler by his supporters. Khan Bahadur Sahib of Sebujni, by leaving the bloc led by his FaBr, Taj Mohammed Khan, and joining the Badshah, gained dominance over lower Sebujni. The power of the Darmei and Babuzai Khans was reinforced in their respective areas.

In an attempt to check the power of the newly appointed head of Swat, Jamroz Khan of Babuzai and most of his allies then shifted their allegiance to Shirin Sahib, the Badshah's brother and only remaining collateral. However, the Badshah put Shirin Sahib in command of a small party of men stationed on the Dir border, and he was killed during an attack by the Dir forces, who were subsequently routed by a large force of Swatis under the command of the Badshah.

In 1926 Swat State was recognized by the British, and the Badshah given the title of Wali and an annual subsidy. By this time, only a few very prominent Khans remained who could rival him in power. These were soon reduced through factional struggles, and the Badshah gained undisputed control of Swat.

---

[1] This account is based on the *History of Swat* previously cited, on the statements of numerous informants, and on references in various works cited in the bibliography, which are of little value as independent sources.

Nevertheless, the organization of local leaders in opposed blocs continued, as did attempts to limit the Badshah's powers by supporting his rivals. His main deputy, Hazrat Ali Khan (of Chitrali descent), and his son and heir, Jahanzeb, became the spearheads of the opposed blocs. The defeat of the heir's bloc in 1935 led to his enforced absence from the State for some time; but later similar intrigues drove a wedge between the Badshah and Hazrat Ali, leading first to the recall of the heir, later to his appointment to control of the State Army in 1943, and finally to the banishment of Hazrat Ali and his brother in 1944. In 1949 the Badshah abdicated so as to devote his whole time to religious pursuits, and Jahanzeb became Wali, appointing his senior son as heir. Even abdication of the Badshah is interpreted by some sceptics as a ruse to trap the enemies of the dynasty by tempting them to make use of the apparent disunity between father and son. The strong current of pro-Pakistani sentiment led the new Wali to make many concessions, both internal and external, which culminated after I left the country in the partial incorporation of Swat in the administered territories of Pakistan.

THE ORGANIZATION OF SWAT STATE

The formal organization of Swat State may be summarized under the three topics of administration, army, and finance.[1]

There is no systematic separation of judicial and executive powers, and no fixed division of responsibilities between departments. The Ruler claims absolute power, and conceives of his administration as 'a family concern' in which duties and responsibilities are informally delegated, at his pleasure, to trusted individuals.

The State is divided into thirty-five *Tahsils*, or local districts, each administered by an appointed *Tahsildar* and an appointed *Qazi* (judge) who is consulted at the discretion of the *Tahsildar*. Groups of *tahsils* are united under seven *Hakims*. *Tahsildars* and *Hakims* are responsible to one of the three *Mashirs* of Upper Swat, Lower Swat and Kohistan, and Buner respectively, who are in constant consultation with the Ruler. Information and appeals travel upwards in this hierarchy, while instruction and decisions are passed downward and implemented by it. The personnel of this organization are civil servants, many of them of Saint caste; they are frequently transferred and rarely permitted to serve in their native area.

The traditional descent group segments and their areas are also recognized, and their leaders, formally recognized as Khans and Maliks, form a second hierarchy of administration. They may be acclaimed by the landowners of their group or selected by the Ruler; except in very special cases they are the leaders of local alliance blocs which, with some support from the centre, are able to dominate the area. Thus if a Khan loses his local following, the Ruler is forced to recognize the leader of the rival bloc as Khan. This is because judicial and executive powers are exercised by the

[1] The description refers to the period of my fieldwork in 1954.

Khans over their areas, and they must themselves supply the coercive force necessary to exercise such powers. Information and appeals pass upward through this hierarchy to the Ruler, but minor executive decisions are taken autonomously. Appeals may however also shift from one framework to the other; an appeal from the decision of a *Tahsildar* may be taken to a Khan, and vice versa.

Special agents are also distributed throughout the area and report to regional superiors. Needless to say, this third framework is not overt.

Relations between local administrators in these differing frameworks are generally strained, and characterized by opposition and an approximate balance of power. The Ruler clearly manipulates the organization to maintain such a balance.

The police forces permanently on duty, which are distributed between eighty fortresses in different parts of the State, have a strength of two thousand, and are controlled by the *Tahsildar* in the *Tahsil* where they are stationed. The Army numbers about ten thousand, only a part of whom are active at any one time. The supreme command, under the Ruler, is held by the *Sipah-Salar*; the present incumbent combines this post with the office of Mashir of Upper Swat. He is the son of the Mian of Ser (p. 128), and is supported by two commanders—his own son, and Pir Mohammed Khan of Babuzai (p. 113). The Army is used extensively for public works. Officers and men hold contracts whereby in return for annual payments in grain they are called on to serve for six weeks in every year, the officers as overseers, the men as labourers, particularly in road and bridge building. Army commissions may be held by Khans but not by *Tahsildars*. Only the supreme commander may order mobilization. As the members of the army resident in any one district are about equally split between the opposed blocs, no local officer can mobilize them on his own authority; thus prospective rebels are effectively prevented from using the Army organization. The private bodyguard of the Wali and the Badshah form separate groups under their own officers.

The finances of the State are administered, on behalf of the Ruler, by the *Wazir-i-Mal*; the present incumbent (brother of Pir Mohammed Khan, the Commander) combines this post with the office of Mashir of Buner. He is assisted by a treasurer and a small staff. The main income of the State derives from a tax of two thirteenths of all agricultural produce. The right to collect this tax in each area is auctioned by the finance minister through the local *Tahsildars*. The person who buys tax rights is given no assistance in collection; in other words, he must command sufficient authority to control the area. Bids are thus made only by politically powerful persons, usually the leaders of local blocs. If unable to collect the amount expected, they have to make up the difference; if they collect more, they retain the excess. Complaints by landowners who claim to have had more than the legal two thirteenths extracted from them are directed to the *Tahsildar*. The bulk of the grain thus collected is stored in regional depots and paid out locally in salaries to army, police, and administrative personnel.

Finally, the existence of several specialized branches of the State organization should be mentioned, such as the extensive and growing educational system and an expanding free medical service.

The *Ruler* himself is assisted by a Chief Secretary and a Private Secretary, and holds daily court, where he may be approached by any subject. His decisions automatically overrule those of others. He is, furthermore, in constant telephonic communication with administrators in the districts. One of the first acts of the Badshah after his election as Ruler was the construction of telephone lines from the capital to the main local centres. The radial pattern of construction offered the further advantage that while he had direct communication with every place, persons in the different centres could not communicate with each other without his knowledge. Roads have also been constructed to give direct access to all areas.

The central political position of the Ruler is thus reinforced by his central location in the system of communications. Furthermore, he maintains the centralized political pattern without having to vest absolute local powers in any single hierarchy of officers. As well as by requiring frequent consultations by telephone, he systematically balances the persons in authority in any one area against each other. Locally dominant leaders are recognized and their powers made use of, for example in collecting taxes. Since the rivalry between blocs is expressed by competitive bidding at the tax auctions, the profits made by leaders from tax rights are apt to be small. The Army, which can be mobilized only from the centre, constitutes the final sanction against leaders. Moreover the Ruler maintains a rough balance between the blocs by supporting now one and now the other. The powers of the Khans are offset also by those of the appointed administrators, such as the *Tahsildars*—who are transferred frequently to prevent collusion with local leaders. Their local powers of subversion are further limited by their dependence on the local police officers—independently appointed by the Ruler—for actual force. Finally, the execution of this policy to the extent that it is not actually in the hands of the Ruler, is delegated to a small number of trusted persons, at present five (Sipah Salar, Wazir-i-Mal, Mashir of Lower Swat, Chief Secretary, Private Secretary), who though in part responsible for different divisions of the State all reside permanently in Saidu Sharif with the Ruler. And as an additional check (besides the net of 'secret' informants) this whole administrative apparatus may at any time be by-passed through a personal appearance at the Ruler's court—though an unsuccessful appeal to this court generally implies uncomfortable consequences for the applicant.

Only in the area of Sebujni/Shamizai, mainly Lower Sebujni, has this system broken down. Previous policy has placed the Ruler in a position where he is forced to continue supporting one Khan. The Hakim dispatched to the area now works in close co-ordination with the Khan, who is said to oppose the Hakim's transfer. An appeal a few years ago by a number of landowners was punished by severe beating with the rifle-butts of the Ruler's bodyguard, and thus cost most of the pleaders their front teeth—enough to make them feel they had got off easy without encouraging them to try again. But though the local Khan thus wields autonomous power within his own area, he is in no position to challenge the Ruler's wider authority.

Otherwise, the traditional system of opposed blocs, maintaining balance by occasional changes in allegiance, continues. None of the factors contributing to it are removed by the State organization. The pre-requisites for local dominance are the same as in the acephalous system. The centralized system is merely superimposed on this, presupposing rather than attempting to replace it. The description of the bloc organization thus remains valid and accurate within the area of Swat State as well as outside its boundaries. The State is maintained on this basis only through the continual activity of the Ruler—mainly by the frequent transfer of *Tahsildars* and recurrent transfers of support from one to the other local bloc. The Army, organized in such a way that only the Ruler can mobilize it, provides the basis for his position of supremacy. But the importance of communications can hardly be overemphasized, particularly in the earlier period when the Army was weaker. The innovation of rapid communications—with the Ruler located in the centre of a radial system of telephone lines and roads—gave him a crucial initial advantage, and may in great measure have been the cause of his success, in founding a viable state organization.

I I

Conclusion

THE MIDDLE EAST is the homeland of states and empires; it has known centralized political systems far longer than any other region of the world (Childe, 1934). The tribal peoples that are found in the region do not retain their tribal institutions through ignorance, but as a stable and successful adaptation to the natural and social environment in which they find themselves. Coon (1952) contrasts these tribal 'Lands of Insolence' with the administered, settled lands of the centralized states, and emphasizes how both have their place in the history and constitution of the Middle East.

Pathans contrast the administered lands with an organized government (*hukomat*) with the lands of freedom and rebellion (*Yaghestan*). In the present study I have tried to analyse the political system in one land of freedom and rebellion.

The point of departure was offered by Schapera's emphasis on the role of leaders and the functions of leadership in political systems. In Swat the groups which constitute the elementary corporate units in the political system are all based on the principle of individual captaincy. There is thus a single leader for each group; and the sources of his authority derive from the whole range of his relations to his followers. When classified in terms of these relations, the leaders fall into two main categories: Pakhtun chiefs, and Saints of holy descent. The former base their authority mainly on wealth and conquest, the latter on their mediatory role and law. Both are clearly political, in that they organize and command their followers, and in the final instance both maintain their authority by resort to force.

The presence of these two different kinds of leader poses a problem, the solution of which is one of my main themes. Though to an outsider chiefs and Saints may appear similar in many respects, they are best understood in conceptual terms as polar complements; the political activities of each presupposes the presence of the other. These two points deserve some elaboration.

Pride, rivalry and virility is expected of chiefs: such behaviour the Pathan villagers remember, encourage and admire. But these characteristics are relative, and are most clearly conceptualized in terms of their opposites: moderation, reasonableness and meekness. This complementary type of behaviour is expected of Saints, and the opposition is carried through to a remarkable extent—for example in the spectacular hospitality of chiefs as opposed to moderation bordering on miserliness among Saints, or in the immaculate white clothes of Saints in contrast to the showy brightness of the garments of many chiefs.

This complementarity is very intimately connected with the difference and interdependence of political roles. The chiefs are members of localized Pakhtun descent groups; they build up their followings and become the leaders of a series of homologous localized men's house groups in a segmentary, acephalous system. The techniques whereby chiefs compete for power tend to create and increase tensions; the opposition between two chiefs tends towards a mounting intensity of violence.

But the same persons who form the followings of chiefs, and admire and support the kinds of behaviour that produce these tensions, are also the followers of Saints. Moreover, the groups led by Saints tend to cut across those of chiefs, and the following of a Saint is generally much more widely dispersed than that of a chief. In most situations where conflicts arise between chiefs, their conceptual counterparts, the moderate, reasonable and pious Saints, intervene. Their prime political role is that of mediator, and they are continually active in arranging compromises and reducing tensions which the chiefs are unable themselves to resolve. The pattern of behaviour whereby chiefs create their followings and compete for dominance within an area would lead to complete anarchy unless the Saints were also active at the same time. Each presupposes the other, and the political system is the resultant of the activities of both.

The basic feature of this system is the alignment of all leaders and their followings into two dispersed, politically corporate blocs of allies. The composition of each bloc, containing both chiefs and Saints, reflects the complementarity between them. Other features of organization also effect the structure of the blocs, notably the strong opposition that tends to characterize the relationship between collateral kinsmen. This opposition within the patrilineages of the dominant landowners leads to the political fission of such groups, and the alignment of the resulting two splinters in opposed blocs. The balance within the Swat segmentary system is thus not maintained by the situational fusion and fission of segments on different levels, as has been described in so many segmentary societies, particularly in Africa. On the contrary, the opposition between rivals in the political system of Swat tends to be permanent; and balance is maintained by a process of growth and ultimate fission of the groups led by single leaders, accompanied by defections from one bloc to the other.

In this book, I have not been able to treat adequately the various problems arising out of this, such as the reasons for the development of no more than *two* blocs, or the meaning of descent in the various sections of this plural society. Nor was it possible to give more than the briefest summary of the developments that have led, within the present generation, to the establishment of a state ruled by a Saint in one part of the valley, and the expansion of the formerly small Khanate of Dir, ruled by a Pakhtun

CONCLUSION 135

chief, into another part, leaving only a small remnant with an unmodified acephalous organization. I can only suggest that these developments are mainly the results of a rearrangement of the traditional elements of organization, combined with the introduction of a few new elements, and some technological innovations, mainly the telephone. Though these new developments give to their areas the appearance of highly centralized states, the basic form and importance of the traditional bloc organization has not yet been changed. However, the founder of Swat State is still alive, though he has been succeeded as Ruler by his son; and the stability of the State has not yet been put to the test, nor is there any evidence that its internal organization has attained an equilibrium.

APPENDIX
Cases Relating to Blood Revenge

CASE 1:

Sayyid of Biha vs. Pacha of Nalkot; Saints of two neighbouring villages in upper Sebujni, c. 1925.

The Sayyid of Biha reaped fodder from a certain G.M.'s fields; he was surprised and beaten by G.M. and his skull was fractured. People egged him on, teasing him for having been beaten, and that by a man so short of stature as G.M. The Sayyid therefore surprised G.M. once in Biha and beat him with the aid of fellow villagers. G.M. then wanted revenge; he waited by the path in the valley bottom, managed to catch two of the Sayyids, and tried to shame them by removing their trousers. In self-defence the Sayyid of Biha slashed G.M.'s stomach open with a knife; he was then caught and tied up. Next morning G.M. died. His son was still a child, and his adult close agnates did not dare take revenge. The more distant relatives were offered the chance of revenge, but hesitated on the ground that they were not closely enough related. So Nalkot Pacha, the brother's son of the murdered man, shot the captive murderer. Later Khan Bahadur Sahib supported Nalkot Pacha's group; they raided Biha and burnt the Sayyid's crops, but the Sayyids had fled to Dir. After three years they returned on the Night of Sacrifice, and begged pardon of the family, which was then granted.

CASE 2:

Khan Kor vs. Ali Khel; chiefs of Thana, started c. 1910

Groups of young men were playing around at night, teasing each other. Those of Baze ward criticized the leader of the gang in Ali Khel ward. He was insulted; he managed to catch the leader in Baze ward of Khan Kor, remove his pants, and chase him through town. The Khan Kor leader in return laid an ambush, caught the Ali Khel leader on his way to the 10 p.m. Ramazan prayers at the mosque. In the ensuing fight, Ali Khel was killed. A *warbandi* was arranged—i.e. the two groups involved in blood feud were banned by the village council from simultaneously living in Thana village; on alternate years, Khan Kor moved to their colony village of Palai, then Ali Khel moved to Dir. About twenty years passed; finally the brother of the dead Ali Khel killed the Khan Kor murderer on the high road. The Political Agent of Malakand was involved, since the murder was committed on the King's Road. The murderer was sentenced to fourteen years in an Indian prison. During this time, *warbandi* was relaxed. But when the prisoner was released and returned home, the brother and the son of the dead Khan Kor man swore they would still have their revenge, and had their servant shoot the former prisoner in the bazaar. That was eleven years ago; the feud is not regarded as having been concluded yet.

CASE 3:

Khan A vs. Khan B; sons of prominent chiefs at time of fieldwork

Young Khan A was spending the hot months in a hunting shelter in the hills; his friend Khan B came to visit him. At 6 p.m. they went off together, without any servants. In the course of a quarrel between them Khan A pointed his shotgun at B; B managed to push the barrel down but had his leg torn to pieces by coarse shot. B pretended he thought A had been joking and fired by accident; he said, 'you must bandage me and carry me to the hut'. A tried, but his knees turned to jelly with fear; he ran to the hut and had the servants fetch B. They waited till after dark so that no one would surprise them, and then returned to the village to the house of C, A's uncle. While A stood outside, B told the true story of what had happened. A heard this, and fled to the hills, and later to his mother's brother in the neighbouring village. C immediately sent B away, then notified his agnates of what had happened. They all sought refuge in the men's house of C's party ally. Through a mutual relative (sister's husband of C, distant agnate of B) C notified B's father. B's father went heavily armed and escorted to C's men's house and gardens, but could not find him. B had to have his leg amputated. The conflict then gained political content: the feud was used to get at C, whose political influence had been increasing at the expense of that of B's father. Though C publicly repudiated his brother's son's actions, he was unable to divest himself of responsibility. When I left, C was temporarily exiled from his village.

CASE 4:

Tenants of a small village at time of fieldwork

One evening a shot was heard in the fields below the village. Immediately, all fires were put out and armed villagers advanced cautiously towards the place from which the shot had come. After a while, the call 'all clear' was heard, and men carrying torches emerged from some of the houses. A young boy was found dying in the fields. He was carried on a bed up to the house of his sister, who was married in the village; he himself was from the neighbouring village. He said he had been guarding his field when two men came to steal from it. He tried to catch them, but they fired and escaped; he had not recognized them. He bled heavily from a wound in his chest; in the course of the night he died. There were rumours that the boy had disclosed the identity of his attackers. His relatives came to me to borrow an airletter, which I later addressed and had posted for them in the nearest post office, thirty miles away. It supposedly informed the dead boy's brother, who was working in Bombay, of the events and begged him to come home to pursue revenge. A week later, the *Tahsildar* arrested a man for murder, alleging that the boy had supplied the name to his family before dying. The arrested man had been caught twelve years previously attempting to rape the dead boy's mother; he had escaped with a severe beating and left the village, to return only a year ago. The *Tahsildar* pressed the family of the boy to testify against the arrested person, lest their denial of knowledge should invalidate later testimony. So they disclosed the names of two more men, though the dying boy had said there were only two in all. In the meantime, the dead boy's sister's husband moved to his in-laws' house to protect the younger sur-

viving brother-in-law. Next, the chief of the ward of the two last arrested
went down to the *Hakim* in charge of the case, and the two arrested men
were released, while rumours about bribes circulated in the village. The
family of the dead boy later denied having named the two men.

After a while, the rival chief of the other ward of the dead boy's village
went to get the release of the man first arrested. By this time a new version
of the motive was circulating: a fairly prominent Pakhtun had been the
fee-paying tenant (p. 44) of the Khan of a neighbouring village; he sublet
the land in question at a considerable profit. The family of the dead boy
received so much money from his brother in Bombay that they had approached
the Khan outbidding the Pakhtun for tenancy rights. He threatened them to
make them desist, but they pressed on. So the Pakhtun hired the arrested
man to murder the boy—in which case the responsibility would fall on the
Pakhtun, not the arrested man. The case had not been closed when I left the
area.

CASE 5:

Khan D vs. Khan E; prominent chiefs at time of fieldwork

Khan D in his capacity of *jamidar* in the Swat army, was supervising road
repairs in the town of Mingora. Work was being done in front of some houses
belonging to Khan E, his traditional enemy. Khan E started interfering with
the work and re-directing the workmen, and he abused the foreman when
they refused to follow his orders. Khan D arrived on the spot and told the
workman to proceed as before, since E had no authority in the matter.
E persisted, D told him to go away, E lost his temper and slapped D in the face.
It being beneath D's dignity to take part in a common street-brawl, he went
away; E went to the Ruler to ask for protection. The Ruler refused to provide
him with a bodyguard, so he went into hiding. D's younger brother, resident
in another village, leading a group of servants and tenants, managed to find
out where E was, and after four days succeeded in stopping his lorry as he
was getting out of town and overpowering his guard. They pulled him out
on the road and started thrashing him; his skull was cracked and one ear
torn off. For the next twenty-four hours after this D's men's house was
thronged with followers demonstrating their loyalty by sitting there. Khan
D was fined by the Ruler; but his honour had been defended by the action,
and his prestige greatly enhanced.

Bibliography

I. SOURCES RELATING TO THE SWAT VALLEY

BADEN-POWELL, B. H. (1896). *The Indian Village Community*. Longmans, Green & Co., London.

BARTH, FREDRIK (1956). Indus and Swat Kohistan. *Studies honouring the centennial of Universitetets Etnografiske Museum*, vol. II. Oslo.

BARTH, FREDRIK (1959). The system of social stratification in Swat, North Pakistan. In E. R. Leach (ed.) *Aspects of Caste*. Cambridge Papers in Social Anthropology No. 2. Cambridge University Press.

BARTH, FREDRIK and GEORG MORGENSTIERNE (1956). Vocabularies and specimens of some S-E Dardic dialects. *Norsk Tidsskrift for Språkvidenskap*, vol. 18.

BARTON, SIR WILLIAM (1939). *India's North-West Frontier*. John Murray, London.

BELLEW, H. W. (1864). *A General Report on the Yusufzai*. Government Press, Lahore.

BRUCE, R. I. (1900). *The Forward Policy and Its Results*. Longmans, Green & Co., London.

CHURCHILL, W. L. S. (1898). *The Story of the Malakand Field Force*. Longmans, Green & Co., London.

COBB, E. H. (1951). The Frontier States of Dir, Swat and Chitral. *Journal of the Royal Central Asian Society*, vol. XXXVIII.

ELPHINSTONE, HON. MOUNTSTUART (1839). *An Account of the Kingdom of Caubul, and its dependencies, in Persia, Tartary, and India*. 2 vols, 2nd ed. Richard Bentley, London.

FERRIER, J. P. (1858). *History of the Afghans*. John Murray, London.

HAY, W. R. (1934). The Yusufzai State of Swat. *The Geographical Journal*, vol. LXXXIV, no. 3.

History of Swat. A printed but undistributed translation of an Urdu account by the late scribe of H.R.H. Abdul Wadud. Citations are based on notes made while reading this work.

KHAN, GHANI (1947). *The Pathans*. National Information & Publications Ltd. Bombay.

MORGENSTIERNE, GEORG (1927). An Etymological Vocabulary of Pashto. *Det Norske Videnskaps-Akademi i Oslo* II, Hist.-Filos. Klasse, Nr. 3.

Papers re British Relations with Neighbouring Tribes on the North-West Frontier of India. *Parliamentary Papers*, Cd. 496, 1901.

PLOWDEN, T. C. (1875). Selections from the Tarikh-i-Murass'a of Afzal Khan, c. 1700 A.D., in: Translations of the Kalid-i-Afghani. Central Jail Press, Lahore.

RAVERTY, H. G. (1860). *A Grammar of the Pukhto.* 2nd ed. Williams and Norgate, London.

RAVERTY, H. G. (1867). *A Dictionary of the Pukhto.* 2nd ed. Williams and Norgate, London.

RIDGEWAY, R. T. I. (1918). *Pathans.* Handbooks for the Indian Army. Calcutta.

ROBERTSON, SIR GEORGE SCOTT (1899). *Chitral—the story of a minor siege.* Methuen & Co., London.

STEIN, SIR AUREL (1929). *On Alexander's Tracks to the Indus.* Macmillan & Co., London.

STEIN, SIR AUREL (1930). An Archaeological tour in Upper Swat. *Memoirs of the Archaeological Survey of India,* No. 42, Calcutta.

WYLLY, H. C. (1912). *From the Black Mountain to Waziristan.* Macmillan & Co., London.

ZABEEH, MOHAMMAD ISMAIL (1954). *Glimpses of Swat.* Ferozsons, Peshawar.

II. ANTHROPOLOGICAL WORKS CITED

BARTH, FREDRIK (1953). Principles of Social Organization in Southern Kurdistan. *Universitetets Etnografiske Museum Bulletin No. 7.* Oslo.

BOHANNAN, LAURA (1952). A genealogical charter. *Africa,* vol. XXII.

CHILDE, V. GORDON (1934). *New Light on the Most Ancient East.* Kegan Paul & Co., London.

COON, CARLETON S. (1952). *Caravan : The Story of the Middle East.* Jonathan Cape, London.

EVANS-PRITCHARD, E. E. (1949). *The Sanusi of Cyrenaica.* Clarendon Press, Oxford.

FIRTH, RAYMOND (1951). *Elements of Social Organization.* Watts & Co., London.

FIRTH, RAYMOND (1954), Social Organization and Social Change. *Journal of the Royal Anthropological Institute,* vol. 84.

FORTES, MEYER (1945). *The Dynamics of Clanship among the Tallensi.* Oxford University Press.

FORTES, MEYER (1949). *The Web of Kinship among the Tallensi.* Oxford University Press.

FORTES, MEYER (1953). Structure of unilineal descent groups. *American Anthropologist,* vol. 55.

FORTES, MEYER, and E. E. EVANS-PRITCHARD (1940). *African Political Systems.* Oxford University Press.

DE JOUVENEL, BERTRAND (1945). *Power; the natural history of its growth.* Hutchinson & Co., London.

LINTON, RALPH (1936). *The Study of Man.* Appelton-Century Co., New York.

MAINE, SIR HENRY SUMNER (1861). *Ancient Law.* John Murray, London.

MARWICK, M. C. (1952). The social context of Cewa witch beliefs. *Africa*, vol. XXII.

PATAI, RAPHAEL (1949). Musha'a tenure and co-operation in Palestine. *American Anthropologist* vol. 51.

RADCLIFFE-BROWN, A. R. (1935). Patrilineal and matrilineal succession, *reprinted in: Structure and Function in Primitive Society*, Cohen & West Ltd., London 1952.

SCHAPERA, I. (1956). *Government and Politics in Tribal Societies*. Watts, London.

STEVENSON, H. N. C. (1954). Status evaluation in the Hindu caste system. *Journal of the Royal Anthropological Institute*, vol. 84.

WEBER, MAX (1947). *The Theory of Social and Economic Organization* [translated by A. R. Henderson & Talcott Parsons]. William Hodge & Co. Ltd., London.

WISER, W. H. (1936). *The Hindu Jajmani System*. Lucknow Publishing House.

Index